Subhadra Sen Gupta (1952–2021) wrote over forty books for children because she thought children are the best readers in the world. In 2014, she was awarded the Bal Sahitya Puraskar by the Sahitya Akademi. In 2020, she won the Big Little Book Award instituted by Parag—An Initiative of Tata Trusts.

Also by Subhadra Sen Gupta in Talking Cub

A Clown for Tenali (2020)
Mostly Ghostly Stories (2019)
The Teenage Diary of Jahanara (2019)
The Teenage Diary of Jodh Bai (2019)

The Story of the First Civilizations

From Mesopotamia to the Aztecs

SUBHADRA SEN GUPTA

Illustrated by Devashish Verma

talking CUB

An Imprint of Speaking Tiger Books

TALKING CUB

Published by Speaking Tiger Books LLP
125A, Ground Floor, Shahpur Jat,
Near Asiad Village, New Delhi 110 049

First published in paperback in Talking Cub
by Speaking Tiger Books in 2021

ISBN: 978-93-5447-169-8

eISBN: 978-93-5447-174-2

10 9 8 7 6 5 4 3 2 1

Typeset in Spectral by Jojy Philip

Printed at Shree Maitrey Printech Pvt. Ltd., Noida

Contents

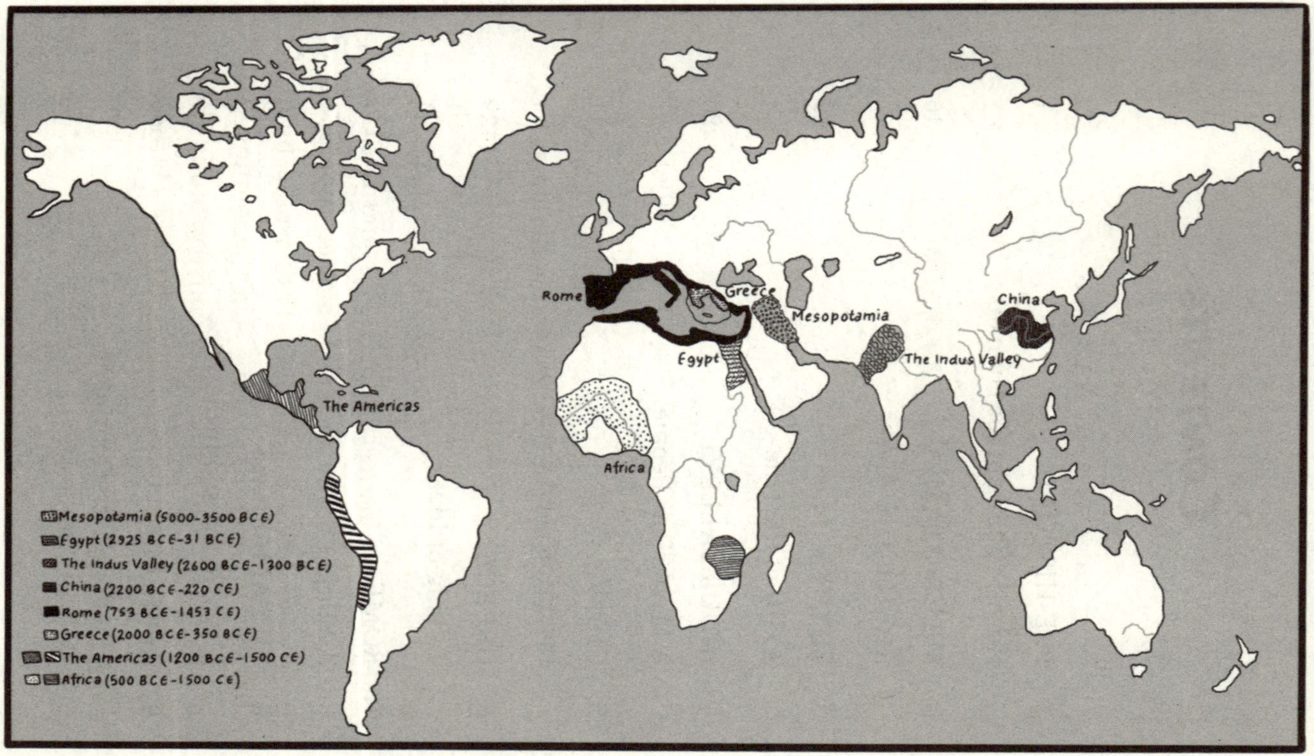

The first civilizations of the world

PRE-HISTORY

How It All Began for Humans

Our human ancestors—the Homo sapiens—first wandered the earth 2,00,000 years ago. In the following millenniums, as their brains developed, they did some pretty remarkable things. Perhaps because of that, in 1758, Carl Linnaeus named the species Homo sapiens. In Greek, *homo* means human and *sapiens* is someone who is wise, sensible and judicious.

The story of civilizations is about how the species that once lived in forests, hunting animals and gathering fruits and berries would one day build cities, weave cloth, make pottery, compose poetry, sing and play drums. They would build highways, palaces and ships. They would invent mathematics and discover chemistry; study the sun, stars and planets and also tell jokes. One day they would print books, invent computers, land on the moon and also act in cinema.

What makes us humans unique is that we have language, science, culture and engineering—things civilizations create. Civilizations have given us political systems like democracy and philosophies like the thoughts of the Buddha and Confucius. And don't forget, Sapiens are the only living species in our solar system to have developed a multitude of civilizations, from Mesopotamia to the Aztecs. How Sapiens became civilized makes for a fascinating story.

A New Kind of Ape

Let's talk of apes because they are our ancestors after all. We share our DNA with chimpanzees, orangutans and gorillas. So even though we are very evolved and smart apes, we are still *apes*! If you want to go on believing that an old gent with white hair and a flowing beard (and at times four hands) called God, Brahma or Zeus waved a magic wand and created humans, you are welcome to do so, but scientists do not agree. And most importantly, anthropologists have found proof of our ape-like ancestors. These are ancient bones called fossils—including whole skeletons—and remains of ancient tools that not only prove Sapiens descended from apes but also that after many thousands of years, we became very different from them.

Sapiens trace back their line to the chimpanzee, and anthropologists think that around six million years ago, a chimpanzee mother had two daughters. One carried on with the chimpanzee line and the other began the line of the Homo species. There were several Homo lines like the Homo erectus, Homo neanderthal and Homo habilis and they gradually began to differ from the apes. The first big change was that they began to walk upright on their hind legs and that freed their hands to hunt animals. Then their agile thumbs meant they could carve tools and build fires. Once they learned to make fire, they could cook meat and grains on the fire and this improved their diet, and better nutrition meant sharper brains. Sapiens are the last of the Homo line, coming just after the Neanderthals and they appear 2,00,000 years ago. For a while, they shared the forests with other Homo species like the Neanderthals but by about 30,000 years ago, most of the other Homo line had become extinct.

We Think and We Talk

Two crucial things happened that took the humans away from the animal world: the scientists call them the Cognitive and the Agricultural Revolutions. We learnt to talk, we created a writing script and then we learnt to grow crops.

First, humans learned to communicate with each other and created a spoken language. Now you will say, 'So what's new, all animals talk to each other.' True. Birds chirp, lions roar and dogs bark but human language is much more intricate because we have words and sentences. This is because somehow our brains became wired differently and we developed words to describe our world by giving things names. Something like, 'That yellow fruit is sweet and delicious, and I'll call it banana.' Or looking up and thinking, 'That blue top above is the sky and those white and fluffy things floating up there are clouds.'

Soon we began to string words into sentences and then started to share information, express our emotions and also gossip. And today, everything from school to working in an office to sharing a recipe requires that we talk. This Cognitive Revolution began in our minds and this is what we call language. We are unique because we can speak in hundreds of tongues with millions of beautiful, expressive, descriptive words. And we are still creating new words and every new generation has its own lingo—what we call slang. When your grandparents were young, they did not know words like hip-hop, sneakers or Instagram, and you never use words they did like telegram, water carrier or fountain pen! That is the magic of language.

The next stage of the Cognitive Revolution was crucial because now we developed a written script and learnt to write everything down—and we have not stopped writing since. We kept records, wrote letters, printed books and now we WhatsApp and email. This was the first step to creating a history of a people. All this writing recorded the details of not just kings and battles, but also about gods and goddesses; what we ate and the clothes we wore; our songs and our games. It is about our daily lives and the events of the world. And that, my friend, is what we call history.

Baking Bread and Brewing Wine

The second big development began in the area that covers modern Iraq, Syria, Jordan and stretches south to Egypt. Historians call this region the Fertile Crescent. This is where humans began to grow crops by the banks of three rivers—the Tigris, the Euphrates and the Nile—and this is the start of the Agricultural Revolution. Till then, humans were hunter-gatherers, wandering the forests gathering fruits, herbs, roots and wild grasses and also hunting animals. It was a nomadic life as they moved around the land searching for food.

Around 12,000 years ago, humans learnt to plant and grow crops which became the next step towards building a civilization. To grow crops, you have to first plant the seeds, then tend the plants and harvest the crops, which meant you would have to stay in one place. So, humans built simple huts near their fields and soon these became villages. Here the potter made pots, the weaver wove cloth and the farmer tended his fields. One day, villages led to the building of towns and cities, and that was where civilizations began.

From the Big Bang to Cities

- 13.5 Billion years ago: The Big Bang
- 4.5 Billion years ago: Planets appear
- 3.8 Billion years ago: Living organisms appear
- 300 million years ago: Dinosaurs walk the earth
- 6 million years ago: The great apes live in Africa
- 2.5 million years ago: The genus Homo evolves

- 2 million years ago: The Homo family moves out towards Asia and Europe
- 5,00,000 years ago: Neanderthals appear in Europe
- 3,00,000 years ago: They learn to use fire efficiently
- 2,00,000 years ago: Homo sapiens appear in East Africa
- 70,000 years ago: Sapiens develop language and begin to move out of Africa
- 45,000 years ago: Sapiens reach Australia
- 16,000 years ago: Sapiens reach North America
- 12,000 years ago: Sapiens develop agriculture
- 10,000 years ago: Sapiens are the only Homo species left on earth

So What's a Civilization Anyway?

The word 'civilization' comes from the Latin word *civitas* or city and a *civis* is a citizen, so it is connected with the life of cities. Of course, that does not mean that people living in villages were not part of a civilization. It just means a people that lived in both villages and cities, and their lives were intertwined, much in ways in which they are today, and that formed a civilization. A city does not produce food, a village cannot manufacture bicycles or mobile phones; so they share and sell through trade and soon this trade spreads to other cities and beyond that to other civilizations.

A civilization begins with a network of cities that share a similar life and culture. It has people living in planned localities with roads, houses, palaces, temples, offices and markets. These people often have a ruler and a government of ministers and officials; there are laws that everyone obeys; an army and also a police; people follow one or different religions, and there are priests; and it has a unique culture of literature, music, dance, architecture, painting, sculpture, handicrafts and handlooms. Even the food we eat—the unique recipes of each region—is a part of a culture. Without a civilization, life would be just about gathering or hunting for food, eating, sleeping, having babies and fighting. Cats, dogs, chimpanzees and elephants—all do that. With civilizations, we have created something complex and unique in our solar system.

BC and AD or BCE and CE?

We will use dates with the abbreviation of BCE or CE after the numbers. Earlier, this used to be

BC and AD. This is because the international calendar was developed in Europe and the dates began with the birth of Jesus Christ. So BC was 'before Christ' and AD was '*anno domini*' in Latin or 'after Christ'. Now it has been simplified to BCE or 'Before the Christian Era' and CE or the 'Christian Era'.

It is a bit confusing because the BCE years move backwards. So King Ashoka who became king in 268 BCE did so 268 years before the birth of Christ. Mahatma Gandhi was born in 1869 CE and that is 1869 years after the birth of Christ.

Rivers were crucial for the development of civilizations because without water we could not have grown crops. So the first civilization began by the banks of rivers. The earliest came up along the rivers Euphrates and Tigris around modern Iraq, Syria and Jordan. Today, it is a barren, near-desert area, but in those days it was a fertile and green region where it was easy to grow crops. This area came to be called Mesopotamia, which means the 'land between two rivers' in Greek. Another civilization came up around the same time by the banks of the Indus River in India with cities like Harappa and Mohenjodaro: the Indus Valley Civilization. And the third grew by the

River Nile in Egypt. These three—Mesopotamia, Egypt and India—were the first civilizations in the world and China followed soon after.

What was so special about Mesopotamia? This was where humans started agriculture and, in a leap, moved from being nomads to people who lived in one place all year. Anthropologists think agriculture, or the growing of crops, was discovered by women who gathered wild grasses like wheat and realized that when the seeds fell to the ground they sprouted again. Also, unlike vegetables, fruit or meat, grain can be stored for a long period. So they began to plant seeds and tend them as crops but to do that they had to stay at the same place, and thus, villages appeared. Then they invented the wooden plough to till the land and sickle to cut the crop and began to grow larger crops. Some people began to make the tools needed for daily life: they moulded pots and pans from clay, and knives and shovels from iron and we got metal workers and potters.

As their crops became larger, the farmers realized that they could not consume all the wheat, barley or vegetables themselves, so they began the barter system. A farmer would say to a potter, 'I'll give you a basket of wheat and in exchange you give me that earthen bowl.' Soon, people built huts around their lands using tree branches and then made bricks with mud which were fired in kilns to make them stronger. These were the first villages. As their agriculture expanded, or they made more pottery, they began to take their produce and goods to exchange in a market. These areas with shops became towns. Some towns became so big that they became cities.

Characteristics of a City

The historian V. Gordon Childe describes cities as being larger and more densely populated than a village. A city has people of different professions—like craftspeople, officials and priests—living in it and people use the farm surplus for food. The city has many public buildings like palaces and temples and the citizens who know how to keep records in writing, use science and technology and calendars. They appreciate the arts like literature, music and dance and profit from long-distance trade.

The remains of the oldest villages have been found in Jericho beside the Jordan River and

Catal Huyuk in Turkey. What is amazing is that Jericho is still a living settlement. Even if we say that a civilization is connected to cities, it really begins in a village where a farmer ploughs, sows and harvests crops that sustain the people in cities. A civilization cannot survive without farmers and as we shall read in the story of the Indus Valley Civilization, when villages die, a civilization dies with them.

The first kingdoms appeared in Mesopotamia around 5000 years ago and the first empire was the Akkadian Empire of Sargon. Here, the first written script appeared; they minted coins and money instead of barter and that helped develop trade. Gods and goddesses were worshipped in temples run by priests. So Mesopotamia is the first civilization in the history of the world. After this, the world burst with development and cities and kingdoms appeared across Asia and North Africa.

There were civilizations in Egypt, India, China and Persia; soon to be followed by Greece, Rome and later the Mayans and Aztec of Mexico and the Incas in Peru. In Africa, we had the kingdoms of Carthage, Nubia, Somalia, Aksum, Mali and Zimbabwe. What is really odd is that we know so much about the civilizations of Asia,

Europe and the Americas but we have somehow forgotten those in the interiors of Africa. It is very puzzling how the continent where the first humans appeared and the whole story of civilizations really began, somehow recedes from history when civilizations rise.

In this book, we will read about the life of the people in the world's earliest and most influential civilizations—Mesopotamia, the Indus Valley Civilization, Egypt, Greece, China and Rome. We will also travel to South America to discover the Mayans, Aztec and Incas and to Africa of the Somalia, Mali and Nubian civilizations.

MORE HOMO SAPIEN FACTS

- We belong to a distinct branch of the family of great apes like the chimpanzee, gorilla and orangutan. Our closest ape relative is the chimpanzee.
- The primitive humans belonging to the Homo genus include Homo erectus, Homo neanderthal, Homo habilis, Homo soloensis, Homo floresiensis, Homo denisova, Homo rudolfensis and Homo ergaster.
- Homo species are often named after the place where their fossil was first found. The

first Neanderthal fossil was discovered in the Neander Valley in Germany.

- The oldest tool, a stone hand axe 2.5 million years old, was found in Ethiopia.
- The last Homo species to become extinct 13,000 years ago was Homo floresiensis. They were dwarfs and their fossils were found in an isolated island in the Indonesian archipelago.
- Among the tools developed by Sapiens were also weapons such as spears, harpoons, bows and arrows.
- The Sapiens got to places as far as Australia and South America. The only place that the Sapiens did not reach was Antarctica.
- During the Agricultural Revolution, wheat and barley were grown first in the crescent of Iraq, Turkey and Syria. Rice and millet were developed in China and India. Many vegetables and fruits like potato, tomato, pineapples and chillies are the gifts of Mexico and Peru.
- The first animal to become a pet was the dog. We see them in cave paintings. Then sheep, goats, cattle and pigs were herded for food and also skins and fur.
- The first cotton textile was woven around 6000 BCE probably in India and the first silk was woven in China. The first potter's wheel was used in Mesopotamia in 4000 BCE. For

thousands of years, Indian cotton textiles would be taken to many other civilizations in Asia and Europe.

- The first drink to be brewed was beer from barley in Mesopotamia. Later, wine was distilled from grapes in Egypt. One wonders what these drinks were called then!

MESOPOTAMIA

BETWEEN TWO RIVERS

(5000 BCE–3500 BCE)

History books will tell you that the first cities in the world appeared in Mesopotamia. Yet, if you travelled back in time and asked the people of these cities where they lived, they would not say 'Mesopotamia'. They would say, 'We live in the city of Ur of the kingdom of Sumer.' Or 'I live in Babylon.'

That is because 'Mesopotamia' is a Greek word that means 'between two rivers' and refers to the Tigris and Euphrates. Greek historians gave the whole region this name many centuries later because they did not know the local language and had no clue what the place was called. Think of Mumbai being called Bombay and Kochi spelled as Cochin by the British. That's what happens when historians from other countries try to write your history—they get all the names wrong.

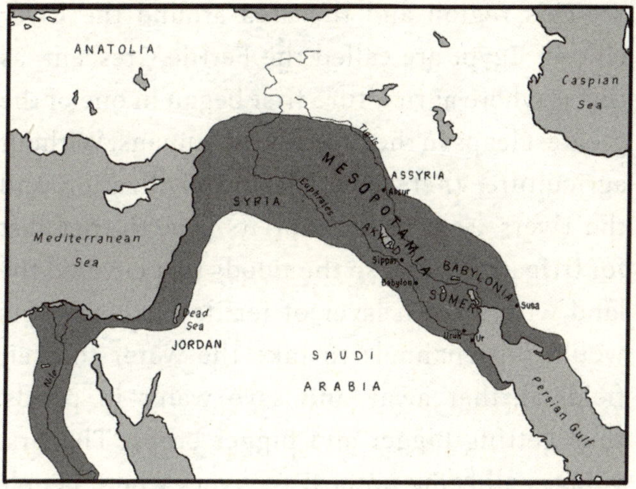

Sumer? Where's That?

The region called Mesopotamia lies between the rivers Tigris and Euphrates in the present-day region of Iraq and spreads across Syria, Jordan, Palestine, Israel and into Turkey. The two rivers originate in the southern mountains of Turkey and flow into the Persian Gulf, which used to be the heart of agriculture in the region. This region that we now see as dry and desert-like was once green and covered in wheat and barley fields, palm trees and apple orchards, but because there was little rainfall, the farmers needed the rivers for irrigating their fields.

This region and the area around the River Nile in Egypt are called the Fertile Crescent, as this is where agriculture first began in one of the greatest leaps in the progress of humans. Without agriculture, there could be no civilization and the rivers were crucial for its growth, not just for irrigation but also the floods that covered the land with a fresh layer of fertile mud. Farmers would dig channels to take the water to their fields further away and save water in ponds, thus getting bigger and bigger crops. The first villages all came up next to rivers where people began to live in houses built of mud brick with straw roofs.

As agriculture developed, the population grew and the farmers began exchanging the surplus wheat or barley for goods like pottery or textiles. That led to the start of markets where people brought their goods. Often near the market, a temple would spring up because people wanted to worship the gods

and goddesses. These markets and temples were at the heart of the rise of towns and then cities. In the cities, people did not grow their own food; they were dependent on the farmers to supply the grain and vegetables to them as they worked as traders, officials, priests or craftsmen.

Instead of labouring in the fields, the people in the cities became the creators of pots and pans, jewellery, clothes, knives and shovels. The artists worked at the temples making paintings and sculptures; poets, singers, dancers and storytellers travelled from village to village entertaining people and these products and services were exchanged for both money and food. Today, people living in cities often look down on farmers but they have been able to survive only because the farmers take care of the crucial work of growing food. It is our villages that make cities possible.

Temple Towns

Towns and markets often grow around large temples because they offer business to shops and craftspeople. As hundreds of pilgrims visit the temples every day, they shop in the markets, eat in the food stalls and stay in the hotels. We still have such pilgrim towns in India like Kanchipuram, Varanasi or Mathura that are filled with temples and are the centres of the local economy. The markets around temples, like the Vishwanath Gali in Varanasi, offer not just flowers and puja material but also sell clothes and metal ware.

The first kingdom in Mesopotamia was called Sumer and the oldest city found so far was called Ur. Sumer was in southern Mesopotamia and another kingdom called Akkad grew in the north. Mesopotamia had many big cities like Uruk, Kish, Eridu and Nippur. However, it doesn't sound quite right calling someone from Ur a 'Mesopotamian', as after all the word did not exist in their language. The people called their land Sumer and spoke in the Sumerian language.

So even though we'll call the civilization Mesopotamia we'll refer to the people by their kingdom or city like Sumer or Babylon, Akkad or Assyria.

City Number One

If you were a villager walking towards the city of Ur, it would have been an amazing sight: the brown mud walls of the city rising above the green wheat fields. And inside, there were narrow lanes lined with double-storeyed homes, bazaars, taverns, palaces and a giant temple. This is where civilization began. Soon there were other cities like Kish, Eridu, Lagash and Nippur and they were all centres of trade. Craftsmen—potters, leather-makers, wood-carvers, weavers—all worked here and farmers brought their crops, cereals, fruits and vegetables to exchange for earthen pots or wooden furniture. Soon people opened shops selling cloth, metal ware and jewellery. They first used copper to make metal ware and then created bronze by mixing it with tin, which was a much harder metal and was used to make knives and swords.

Each city was like a state with its own government and people paid taxes at the temples. The more land people had, the higher was the tax collection. Soon these city-states were fighting

with each other to control the land. During these wars, the man who led the army became very powerful and soon became the king who would rule the city. And when he died his son would take his place, and in this way the system of monarchy began. When one king ruled over many cities, he would build a large kingdom called an empire. The first ruler of an empire was a king of Akkad called Sargon. So, Sargon was the first emperor in the world! He had a thick beard to prove it! At times, nomadic tribes from different regions like the Hittites or Assyrians invaded the region and conquered the cities. Over the centuries, the important kingdoms were those of Sumer, Akkad and then Babylon and Assyria.

Of course, compared to our cities, these cities were quite small. Historians calculate that in the beginning around 25,000 people lived in Ur and that included the king, the nobility, priests, craftspeople and workers.

Let's Go Digging

You may wonder: how can historians write so confidently that the people of Ur had porridge for breakfast? Or that the women wore bangles and necklaces when they went to a party? Did the children have to go to school and sweat over their homework? The cities of Sumer thrived from 5000 to 3500 BCE—around 7000 years ago. Then how did we find out so much about their architecture, the history and the life of the people?

We have to thank a band of historical detectives called archaeologists for that. They picked up their spades and shovels and went digging and discovered the broken walls and basements of homes, palaces and temples. They patiently dug up fragments of pottery and broken metal ware, imagined how they must have looked thousands of years ago, and carefully stuck them together again. To discover how they recover our past, you just have to visit a museum and see what they found in all these ancient sites.

Some of the best places to make such discoveries are inside the tombs of kings, because kings were often buried with all the things that people believed they would need in their afterlife. So there were pots of grain and lentils, furniture,

The entrance to a tomb of a king

clothes, jewellery, musical instruments and even make-up boxes and board games. And another great place to dig, believe it or not, are garbage dumps where archaeologists find all the things used and thrown away by people—broken pans, discarded toys, fragments of clothes and torn shoes. Every find has a story to tell.

We see this across the world in the tombs of royalty, like the pyramids that were built over the tombs of the pharaohs of Egypt. Kings and queens did not like the idea of dying and imagined there is some mysterious heaven where they would go on living and there, they wanted all the comforts of life. So their tombs were packed with food and drink, soft beds and fancy furniture, clothes and jewellery and at times even animals and servants. These tombs also have carvings and inscriptions that tell the history of the kings—which again helped historians to piece together the stories of the people.

In 1922, the English archaeologist Leonard Woolley discovered the tombs of two kings of Sumer called Meskalamdug and Akalamdug who had lived around 2500 BCE. With all the pottery, furniture, gold and silver, there were also the skeletons of seventy-four people who had been buried with them. They must have been courtiers, servants and slaves of the kings; who had all lain down in neat rows, and drank poison and died so that they could go on serving their master even after death. You'll agree, this is going a bit too far to prove your loyalty.

Ziggurat! What Is That?

At the centre of every city was a tall temple called a ziggurat and it was always the highest building in the city. It was built in slowly diminishing layers like a rectangular cake and to reach the chamber that held the idol of the god or goddess, people had to climb many flights of stairs. It was dedicated to the city's most popular god or goddess and at Ur this was Nanna, the moon god.

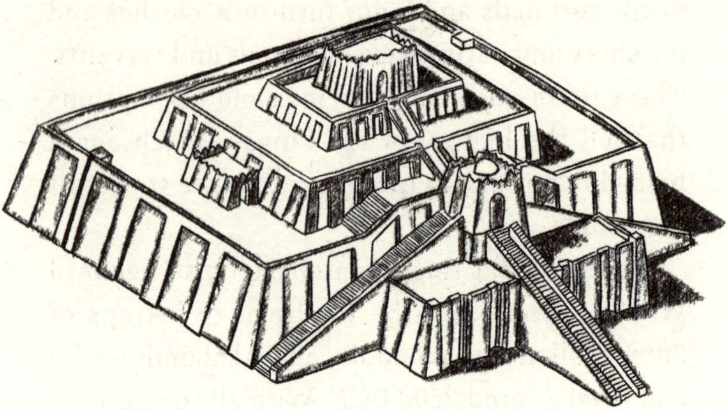

At Babylon it was the mother goddess Ishtar who was also the goddess of war.

The ziggurats, built as artificial hills, are the first temples to be built in the world and are part of the earliest forms of religion. They were surrounded by the quarters of the priests, temple offices and storerooms for grains and other offerings brought by the people. They were always the highest buildings in the city, so people would take shelter there during floods.

Then the priests came up with a clever idea: they told the people that all the land belonged to the gods and that they had to give part of their harvest to him as a sort of tax or rent. When the farmers came to the temple with the god's share of their crops, it was collected by the priests.

They also believed that the gods controlled their lives, so they prayed for rains and good harvests, for good health, and in times of sorrow, they asked the priests to pray for them. The shrewd priests claimed that the gods only listened to them and thus they became very powerful, performing religious ceremonies, reciting the sacred hymns and prayers and happily collecting all the grain.

Goddess Ishtar

The temples were also the centre of the arts and crafts of the city. As many people visited them, dance and musical performances were held in the courtyards, and poets and storytellers gathered an audience around them. In this

A Mesopotamian god

way, temples became centres of culture. Outside the walls of the temple, shops sold clothes and jewellery; food shops served the travellers; and vendors selling flowers and fruits to be offered to the deity during prayers waited for customers.

O Ishtar, Listen to Me!

Every city had its own favourite god or goddess and there were many deities. For Sumerians, Enlil, the god of storms and winds, was the most important as he brought the rains. They claimed that the king of a city was chosen by Enlil. The moon god Nanna was an old man with a blue beard and was married to Ningal, the sky goddess. Their son was the sun god Shamash. Their daughter Ishtar was the goddess of war and rode a chariot pulled by seven lions as she aimed arrows at the enemy. Ishtar was also the goddess of growing things and she brought rich harvests, so she was very popular. In Babylon, there was the magnificent Ishtar Gate that was decorated with blue tiles.

Writing It All Down

After agriculture and the building of cities, the Sumerians' next gift to the world was the art of writing and it was as great a revolution as agriculture. The priests first developed a script that could be written down on clay tablets and from here began our adventure with words. So you have to thank them for all the books that you read like this one.

Why did the Sumerians start to write? Well, it wasn't to write a letter or keep a diary! It was for the rather boring purpose of keeping records and for trade. The first examples of writing in the world are on clay tablets found in Ur and dated to 3300 BCE. It must have started at the temples where people came in thousands to give grain and animals to the gods, and the priests had to keep a record of all that was collected. So the first pieces of writing found scratched on clay tablets said such exciting things as 'ten bushels of wheat and one cow'. No one was writing love letters or rude emails.

Sumerian Proverb

What the farmers had to give to the temple was a form of tax and a Sumerian proverb written on a clay tablet says, 'You can have a lord. You can have a king. But the man to fear is the tax collector.' And it hasn't changed in 7000 years!

Now the early record keepers did not have paper or pen, and definitely not a mouse and a keypad. Instead, they made small, flat tablets in wet clay onto which they carved the information. Once the clay dried, the tablets could be stored away. Many of them have survived for centuries as thousands of these tablets have been found. The first writing was called pictograph. It had pictures for say a sheaf of wheat or oxen and then the numbers received. They were simple drawings made on the clay tablets using a wooden or metal stylus, a pointed pencil-like instrument.

The people who did the writing were called scribes. Drawing a sheaf of wheat or an ox's head took time, so some clever scribe simplified it into symbols and this form of writing was called cuneiform. The alphabet that has letters for the sounds of words that we use today came much later. Soon they developed arithmetic and used addition, subtraction and multiplication and also created a calendar. In the Mesopotamian cities, the scribes hurried around carrying bags of clay tablets and a

One of the earliest clay tablets

stylus like we carry a notebook, a pen or a laptop. We are all scribes today.

Listen to My Story

The first story in the world was also written at Ur. It is called the 'Epic of Gilgamesh' and it is about the adventures of Gilgamesh, the hero and one of the kings of Ur. As it was carved in stone, the story has survived till today. What is intriguing is that in the story, a man with a boat rescues humans and animals after a great flood—similar to the story of Noah's Ark in the Bible.

Cracking the Cuneiform

The pictograph was easy to read because it was all pictures, but cuneiform was symbols—a lot of complex lines and crosses and quite impossible to read. Historians had been trying to decipher cuneiform writing for many years when in 1844 CE, an English army officer, Henry Rawlinson, cracked the code. He found a rock inscription by King Darius of Persia carved in the 5th century BCE in which the same text was written in three different scripts: Old Persian, Babylonian cuneiform and Elamite. Rawlinson worked out the words that spelled 'Darius' and from there he gradually, over many years, deciphered the cuneiform symbols.

Who Wrote First?

Today the British Museum has 1,30,000 clay tablets in its collection and many of them are yet to be studied. This proves that clay was nearly as good as stone to preserve writing. Some historians feel that writing developed independently in Mesopotamia, Egypt, India and China. The Egyptians wrote on papyrus and the Chinese on bamboo paper, but these did not survive as well as the clay tablets did.

How Much for That Hot Pot?

Around 3400 BCE, the Sumerians invented something that totally changed their lives—the wheel. It began as a potter's wheel that could make pots faster and smoother. Then the wheel was attached to a cart. Now, a wheeled cart pulled by a donkey was a better option than loading your goods on the animal's back and walking for miles. Suddenly people had a vehicle that could carry their goods for long distances, so they could trade with other villages and this led to the growth of towns. Soon enough, the kings put wheels on horse chariots and went to war.

At the same time, women began to use flax threads to weave cloth and simple looms were invented. Bales of cloth were carried to cities and exchanged for other goods. These goods were then carried up and down the rivers and finally to ports, to be taken across the seas. Historians believe that many Mesopotamian cities and the Indus Valley civilizations carried on trade by land and across the Arabian Sea 5000 years ago! We know that they traded with the Indus Valley cities because Harappan seals have been found at Ur.

Sumer traded with lands as far away as Egypt and Turkey. Copper came from Oman, silver and lead from Turkey and timber from Syria. They bought lapis lazuli stones used for their jewellery from Afghanistan, and they traded with lands they called Dilmun, Magan and Meluhha. Dilmun was the port of Bahrain, Magan was Oman and Harappa or Mohenjodaro was probably called Meluhha.

Thor Heyerdahl

In 1977, the Norwegian anthropologist Thor Heyerdahl built a large reed boat like the ones used by Sumerians. He named his boat *The Tigris*. Facing stormy winds and high waves, he crossed the Indian Ocean on it, in order to prove that the Sumerians could have had trade relations with the Indus Valley.

Living in Babylon

Mesopotamia was a flat area and did not have much wood or stone, so houses were built with mud brick that were shaped into rectangular blocks and dried in the sun. When brick makers discovered that if you baked them in fire, they became harder and stronger, the buildings became stronger. In India, too, the cities of the Indus Valley like Mohenjodaro and Harappa were built using fire-baked brick. In Babylon they built double-storeyed houses with rooms, a kitchen and a bathroom but because wood was expensive, they had little furniture. People slept on mats on the floor, and they had a few benches and boxes. They owned many kinds of pottery: bowls and plates to eat with; pots and pans for cooking; and large jars to store food grains, water and oil.

The Sumerians ate well. As wheat and barley were the main cereals, wheat was ground and made into bread and barley was made into a nutritious porridge. There were vegetables like onions, leeks, cucumber, many kinds of beans, garlic and lentils. Milk was made into butter and cheese and there was fish from the river and many kinds of meat. Maybe their breads were similar to our rotis, naans and paranthas!

Now, we come to Mesopotamian fashions. The carvings show people wearing a simple piece of cloth draped around their bodies, and at times a skirt-like dress made of sheep wool. Jewellery and make-up boxes have been found in tombs and we know that both men and women lined their eyes with kohl and seemed to paint their face white like a mask and use colour on their lips and eyelids.

And what happened if you fell ill? The doctors used medicines and a lot of guesswork. One cure for an infected leg says: 'Pass through a sieve and then knead together turtle shells, salt and mustard. Then wash the diseased part with good beer and hot water and rub with the mixture. Then rub again with oil and put on a poultice of pounded pine.' So if you hurt your leg, the doctor would go looking for turtles! Really scary!

Women are not mentioned much in the clay tablets and rarely seen in the carvings. Women and children were considered the property of men, but women did have some rights. They could buy and sell houses and run businesses. Tablets record women buying wool, hiring and paying salaries to other women to weave it into cloth and hiring donkey carts to take the cloth to the market. It is only later, in the empire of Assyria that we read of women living in harems.

Mesopotamian man and woman

Magnificent Babylon

Ur has been forgotten but we all remember the legendary city of Babylon mainly because it is often mentioned in the Bible. In 1792 BCE, Hammurabi became the king of Babylon. He was so powerful that he was called the 'King of the Four Quarters'. He is remembered because he was the first king in the world who not only laid down laws that his subjects had to obey but also stated the punishment for people who broke the laws. These 282 laws covered a variety of topics like divorce, wages of labourers and fees for doctors and they were engraved on stone pillars and stone slabs called 'stela'. These pillars were placed around the cities. Some of them have survived till today.

One of the Seven Wonders of the Ancient World—the Hanging Gardens—was at Babylon. The story goes that King Nebuchadnezzar II married Amytis, Princess of Media in modern Iran, and she missed the green fields and orchards of her homeland. So in 580 BCE, Nebuchadnezzar built a terraced garden for her. We have no pictures of course, but the Hanging Gardens were probably built like an artificial hill with brick terraces planted with trees, vines and flower beds. Streams and waterfalls flowed down the terraces to keep the soil wet as hundreds of slaves laboured day and night carrying water from the Euphrates River to the terraces.

Seven Wonders of the Ancient World

- Pyramids of Giza
- Hanging Gardens, Babylon
- Temple of Artemis, Epheseus
- Statue of Zeus, Olympia
- Mausoleum, Halicarnassus
- Colossus, Rhodes
- Pharos lighthouse, Alexandria

Babylon was full of majestic palaces, broad roads for processions and a ziggurat dedicated to the god Marduk. Visitors entered the city through a famous gate decorated with blue tiles called the Ishtar Gate that had blue walls decorated with white figures of bulls and dragons. The gate was named after the goddess Ishtar. The kings of Babylon built a huge empire covering the land from the Persian Gulf to the coast of the Mediterranean Sea. It was the last and longest surviving city-state of Mesopotamia and the city was still there in 323 BCE when the Greek conqueror Alexander the Great died there on his way back to Greece from India.

MESOPOTAMIAN MISHMASH

- In cuneiform, every word, say for oxen or cloth, had to be written differently, so at least 600 signs had to be memorized.
- A lot of information about Mesopotamia can be found in the Old Testament, the first book of the Bible.
- The god of Babylon called Marduk had four eyes and ears to be able to see and hear everything. The priests were also astrologers and many of the zodiac signs were invented by them.
- Sumerians were the first to blend wheat and barley and brew beer. There were nineteen different types of beer and the Sumerian word for beer still survives in the local language. There is a carving showing a group of men holding beer glasses with a musician playing before them. Only a television showing a football match is missing!
- Boys went to school where they used clay tablets on which they learnt to write and do

sums. Some of these tablets, full of spelling mistakes and marked by a teacher, have survived.

- While we use units of ten in our calculations, the Sumerians used the number six, and that has remained in 60 minutes for an hour and 360 degrees in a circle.
- Sumerian astronomers developed a calendar. Their month of twenty-eight days had four weeks of seven days. Their year had twelve months with a few days to spare. They could predict lunar eclipses and worked out the path of the sun.
- Many nomadic tribes settled in Mesopotamian cities. Among them was one called the Hebrews who established the two kingdoms of Judah and Israel around 1250 BCE. The Hebrews later came to be called Jews and as we find in their sacred book the Old Testament, they had kings named Saul, David and Solomon. They were often at war with a tribe they called Philistines that we know as Palestinians. Sadly, 3000 years later they are still at war.
- Many of the ancient archaeological sites of Mesopotamia have been destroyed by war and the soldiers of the Islamic State. The Iraq

Museum at Baghdad, which contained relics from the Mesopotamian, Babylonian and Persian civilizations, was looted during the invasion of Iraq by the United States in 2003.

EGYPT

A GIFT OF THE NILE

(2925 BCE–31 BCE)

A river flowing right through the middle of a desert led to the rise of Egypt. This is the great River Nile that flows south to north; it begins in the central part of Africa, then flows through a desert to finally meet the Mediterranean Sea. It is the longest river in the world, flowing for 6400 kilometres. Every year, the river would flood its banks, bringing a huge pile of black fertile mud, and when the water flowed away this silt would be left behind. In this way, the land along the banks of the river became perfect for growing crops. The land was so fertile that farmers could grow many kinds of crops and soon villages lined the river. The Nile created a huge green oasis in the desert of North Africa where the Egyptian civilization came up. This is why Egypt is called the gift of the Nile.

Egypt was one of the greatest civilizations of the ancient world and also the wealthiest of the

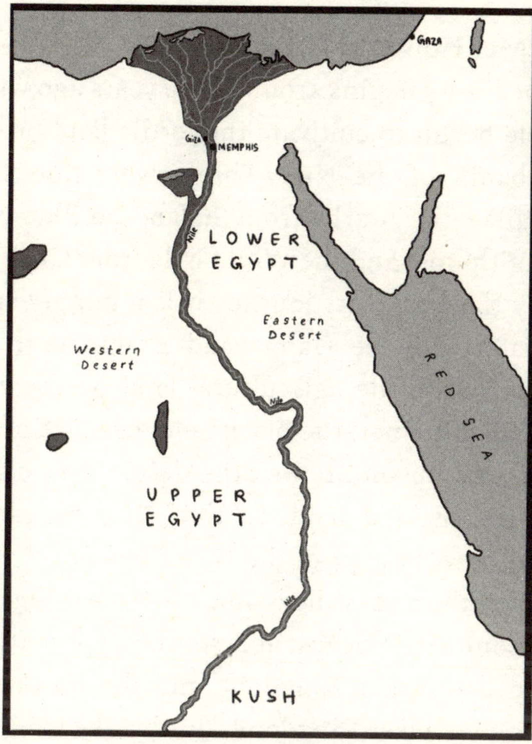

time. It survived for an extraordinary 3000 years, while Mesopotamia and the Indus Valley cities, that began at around the same time, vanished within a few centuries. At least thirty dynasties ruled here and left behind an extraordinary artistic legacy: pyramids, tombs, paintings and sculptures that still dazzle visitors. Who can ever forget the enigmatic Sphinx staring grimly across the desert by the giant pyramids of Giza? Or the gold mask of the pharaoh Tutankhamun?

Tell Me, How Old Is Egypt?

Egypt's story begins around 7000 years ago when people began to cultivate the fertile land on the two banks of the Nile. Three rivers flow into the Nile—the Atarba from Sudan, the Blue Nile from Ethiopia and the White Nile from Ghana—so, by the end of its journey it is a mighty span of water like the Ganga and Brahmaputra in India. The fertile agricultural land by the Nile was called Kemet, the black land, because of the black silt. Beyond it was the desert they called Deshret, the red land. In time, two kingdoms called Lower Egypt of the Nile Delta and Upper Egypt of the river valley came up. Here things get a bit confusing because it is south Egypt that was called the Upper Kingdom, and the north was called the Lower Kingdom! This was because the Nile flows from the south to the north.

In 3100 BCE, King Menes united the two kingdoms and established what came to be known as the first dynasty. Menes also built Egypt's first city that he called Memphis, and he wore the double crown of the two kingdoms. This crown was a combination of the white crown of Upper Egypt and the red crown of Lower Egypt. Wearing two crowns must have given the kings quite a headache and may be that is why the pharaohs usually wore a striped head dress with a snake popping out in front.

An ancient Egyptian tablet representing King Menes

Oh, Great River!

If you look at a map of North Africa, you'll realize that Egypt is like a green oasis surrounded by deserts and it is a land of plenty only because of the Nile. Here farmers grew wheat, cereals, vegetables, dates and cotton. Egypt had three seasons: flooding of the river, planting of the crops and harvest. In spring, the rain and melted snow in the mountains of Ethiopia would swell the Nile with water. The floods would arrive in

July and it was called the inundation because the land was covered in water. The farmers would plant the crops in winter and harvest them in spring and summer. During the flooding season, the farmers would have no work, so they would go off to work for the king who was usually building a tomb or temple. This was their way of paying their taxes to the ruler.

The main cereals were wheat and barley. Flax was grown and woven into linen cloth but cotton was unknown (though today Egyptian cotton is famous around the world). They also grew vegetables like beans, lentils, onions, garlic, lettuce, cucumber, leeks and fruits like melons, grapes, pomegranate, dates and figs. Some of the earliest sweet dishes in the world were made here with dates and honey. We know this because mention of these has been found in ancient papyrus texts.

The Course of a River Changed

In 1971, the Egyptian government inaugurated a giant dam at Aswan. Because of the Aswan Dam, the Nile no longer floods the land and its flow can be controlled but it has created a problem that no one had anticipated. Without floods, that fertile silt is also not deposited by the river and Egyptian farmers are now forced to use chemical fertilizers that are expensive and not environment friendly, proving that most of the time it makes no sense messing with a river.

The Nile was a truly generous river. It brought water for irrigating the fields and silt to make the crops grow for the farmer. The mud was used by potters to make pots and bowls and to make bricks for houses. There were fish and waterbirds that were hunted for food. The river was like a watery highway with boats going up and down. And finally there was the reed papyrus growing along the banks, which was used to build boats and make paper. The desert around the land acted as a protective wall against invasions by enemies and minerals like copper, semi-precious stones, granite and limestone, which were used to build the pyramids, could be found there.

Let's Build a Pyramid

In 2600 BCE, during the rule of the third dynasty, a king named Djoser had a brainwave. He decided that when he died, he wanted to be buried in a big tomb. This was how the first pyramid was built. Djoser thought he would never be forgotten as his magnificent tomb would rise up like a hill

The pyramid at Saqqara

and people would look at it in awe. Now a huge stone building like that was not going to be easy to build but he found an architect named Imhotep who solved the problem. He built it like a stepped hill, a bit like a layered cake, but in the shape of a triangle and not a circle. The Step Pyramid, which is the oldest stone monument in the world, still stands at Saqqara. The problem is that so many pyramids were built later that the Egyptians forgot about Djoser.

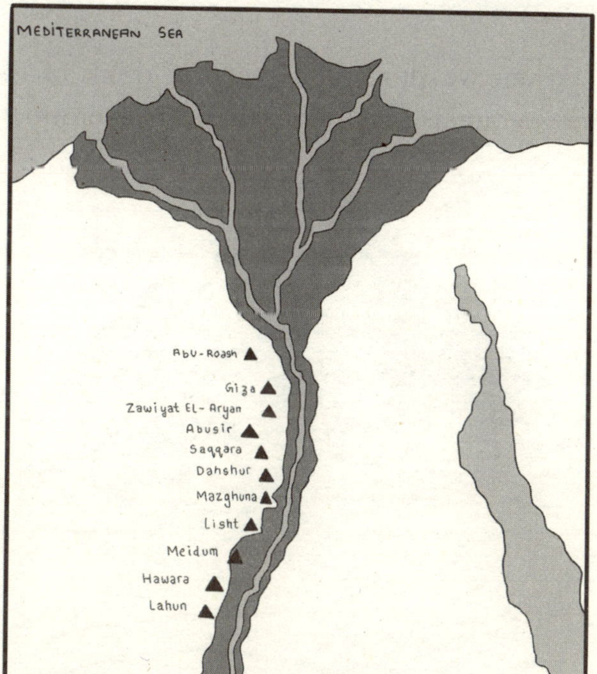

The pyramid fields of Egypt

Imhotep

Even though he was not of royal blood, Imhotep has not been forgotten. He was a remarkable man: an architect who first came up with the idea of a pyramid, a priest, a doctor, an astronomer and an adviser to the king. Later, he was worshipped as a god by people and many of his stone images have survived.

When we think of Egypt, we think of the three pyramids at Giza but there are over ninety

The pyramid at Giza

pyramids still standing along the banks of the Nile, many of them in ruins. The pyramids at Giza were built by the kings Khufu, his son Khafre, and grandson Menkaure. Khufu's pyramid is the tallest. The embalmed bodies of the kings, that we call mummies, were kept in a burial chamber inside, along with many treasures: gold and jewellery, clothes, carvings, paintings, furniture and even chariots, small boats and wooden figures of servants. Though when archaeologists began to explore these three pyramids, they discovered that they had been cleaned out by tomb-robbers centuries ago and all that was left were empty chambers.

Now, why did the kings spend so much to build pyramids and then have their bodies preserved? This was because Egyptians believed in life after death. They enjoyed life so much they wanted to continue with the parties and picnics even after death. So they imagined a heaven where a person lived with the gods. And even in afterlife they would need what they used on earth: food, clothes and servants. The poor, who could not afford fancy tombs, buried their dead in the sand but the rich built tombs, and some of the kings built pyramids. Inside these tombs they buried everything, from fancy furniture, clothes and jewellery to food and even clay images of servants.

Objects found in the tombs

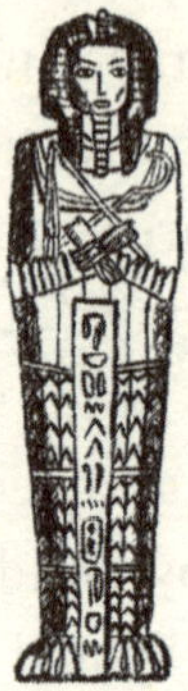

Sarcophagus

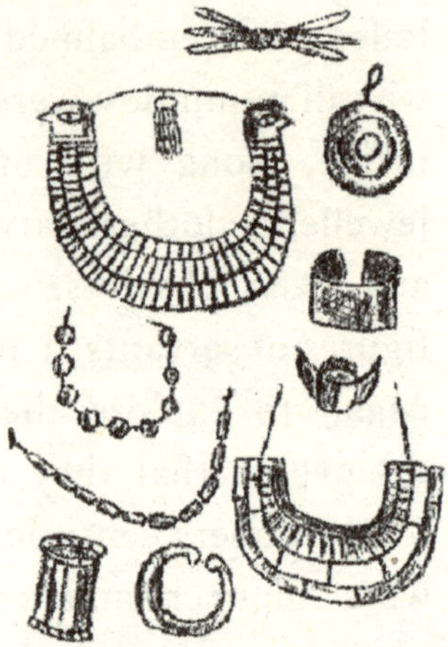

Jewellery

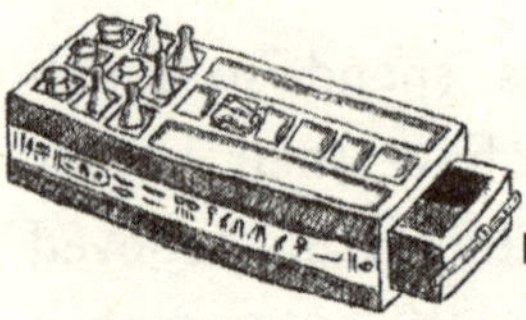

Board games

Wall painting

Oils and ointments

Images of men at war

Food

The largest pyramid at Giza used two million blocks of stone and each weighed about 2.5 tonnes. Have you wondered how they took them to the top? They had no cranes or trucks. What they did was build an earthen ramp that sloped up to the top. The blocks of stone were brought to the site by boat on the Nile and then hundreds of men pushed and pulled the stones tied to ropes. They probably put wooden rollers under the stones to help in all the pulling and pushing. Some later historians said that the kings used slaves for the work but that is not true. The farmers came to work here during the flood season as a way to pay their taxes and they were given places to stay, food and clothing. The craftsmen were paid so well that some of them built their own tombs. The only slaves were prisoners of war and criminals.

Luckily, not all kings built pyramids; or Egypt would have been filled with them. Many of the later kings and queens were buried in tombs built by cutting into hills to create a row of chambers in an area called the Valley of Kings. This was also done because the pyramids had been attacked by tomb-robbers and everything was stolen. In the hope of avoiding robbers, the tombs in the two valleys of kings and queens were cut deep into the hills with hidden entrances and steep passages that were hard to find.

Hey, King Tut!

Over the centuries, most of the treasures in the tombs were looted by grave robbers and many of the mummies vanished. All the grave robbers were not Egyptian. In the 18th and 19th centuries, when Egypt became a British colony, Europeans robbed many tombs and carried off carvings. Egyptian temples had giant carved stone columns standing at their gates that were called obelisks. Today you can see these obelisks in European cities like London and Rome where they were transported by explorers. It was only when archaeologists began to work in the Valley of Kings that the tombs and pyramids were explored and preserved in a proper manner. The Frenchman Auguste Mariette established the Cairo Museum in 1902, and saved the artefacts. Today, the museum attracts thousands of tourists.

For many years, the archaeologists were looking for a tomb that had not been robbed. In 1922, Howard Carter found the untouched tomb of Pharaoh Tutankhamun—the tomb entrance was under a group of old workmen's huts and had escaped the notice of tomb-robbers.

What excited the world the most was the mummy of the pharaoh himself with a solid gold death-mask inlaid with jewels that covered his face. The mummy was laid inside three coffins, the first two of wood and the third made of gold! These coffins were placed inside a stone box called a sarcophagus. And the various chambers in the tomb were stuffed with gorgeous things made of gold, silver and precious stones. There were furniture and a chariot, images of gods and goddesses, jewellery and all the things that Old Tut would need in the afterlife.

Carter's search was funded by a wealthy Englishman named Lord Carnarvon who died soon after the tomb was opened. Thus began the

King Tutankhamun

legend of the 'Mummy's Curse' and the gossip newspapers said that anyone who had touched the mummy had died. In fact, Carnarvon never saw the open tomb or touched the mummy and the people who had actually opened the coffin, including Carter, came to no harm at all! But the story of the mummy's curse continues to live on in books and Hollywood films full of angry mummies flying through the air.

The tombs dug into the hills in the Valley of Kings are amazing places. A narrow opening on the surface leads through a passage into many rooms, the final one being the one where the king's sarcophagus stands. The walls of the passage and rooms are covered in white plaster and paintings showing not just the royal family but also images of daily life in Egypt: women dancing and playing musical instruments; hunters and fishermen; farmers and craftsmen. The most beautiful paintings have been discovered in the tomb of Queen Nefertari. There are also earthen models of ordinary people like bakers grinding wheat, maids carrying baskets and boatmen on the river. This is why we have such a good idea of the life of the people 3000 years ago—it is all preserved by its artists.

The Mysterious Sphinx

The pyramids of Giza are guarded by a giant stone statue called a sphinx. It has the body of a lion and a human head. Many think the face was modelled after King Khafre. Some people believe

the sphinx has magical powers, and the word has entered the English language where a mysterious person is often compared to a sphinx. The nose of the statue is broken and there are many stories about how it happened but no one really knows.

This is the largest sphinx but smaller ones are found around many temples. The one at Giza was carved out of limestone rock and is 73 metres long and 20 metres high. Over the centuries, the pyramids were abandoned and the sphinx was buried in sand up to its shoulders. It was dug out in 1925. Engineers repaired the head that was getting a bit wobbly. The British Museum has a carved piece of stone that was probably the beard of the sphinx but the nose was never found.

O Mighty Pharaoh!

The Egyptian king was believed to be a god on earth and had absolute powers. He was obeyed by everyone. In fact, he was considered so sacred that people never said his name out aloud and when talking of the royal family just referred to the palace. The Egyptian word for palace is 'per ao' and the Greeks turned that into pharaoh.

There were many remarkable pharaohs like Amenhotep I, Akhenaten and Ramesses II who won wars, conquered other kingdoms and built new cities. The longest reign was that of Pepy II, who ruled from the age of six to a hundred years! Some queens were also powerful like Hatshepsut, Nefertiti and Cleopatra, of course. When her husband, the pharaoh Tuthmosis II died in 1473 BCE, Queen Hatshepsut became the regent of the boy king Tuthmosis III who was her nephew. Pretty soon, she took over and crowned herself as pharaoh and sat on the throne holding the royal regalia and wearing the crown as well as a false beard! She was addressed as 'His Majesty' by everyone.

Royal Regalia

If you look carefully at photos of Tutankhamen's mask, he is holding a crook and a flail. The crook is the stick that shepherds carry and this denotes that the pharaoh was like a shepherd of his people. The flail is a whip to punish his enemies. Sometimes pharaohs carry the ankh that looks like a cross with an oval top, and symbolizes life.

Hatshepsut ruled successfully for twenty years, even won some battles and built a magnificent temple. When Tuthmosis III finally took over after her death, he was so angry at having been kept waiting for so long that he tried to wipe Hatshepsut out of history by destroying all her images. Even her temple was demolished and has been recently rebuilt by archaeologists.

Oh Mummy!

You may wonder why the Egyptians were so obsessed with death and afterlife and why did they embalm the bodies of the dead. In those days, the average lifespan of people was around thirty years and people wished that their lives would continue after death. So they imagined another world where they could continue to live and for that they needed their bodies. The bodies were preserved so well that many have survived till today.

The Egyptians believed a person has three souls called the ka, ba and akh and these would survive into the next world. The system of embalming bodies was a long and complicated process. The internal organs were taken out and preserved in jars and the body was covered in a salt called natron to dry it. Then it was stuffed with cloth soaked in oils and resins, sewn up and wrapped in layers of linen bandages. These bandages were covered in more oils and resins and perfumes. The stomach, lungs, intestines and brain were preserved in containers called canopic jars that were placed beside the tomb but the heart was left inside the body because it was believed that the gods judged the person by their hearts.

The whole process of embalming took seventy days and was like a religious ritual. At the end, when the gold mask was placed over the face of the king, the chief embalmer would wear the jackal mask of Anubis, the god of the dead. The whole process meant that Egyptians gained excellent knowledge of the human body.

The oily wrappings soon became thick and sticky almost like tar and the Arab word for tar is 'mumiya'. That is where the word mummy

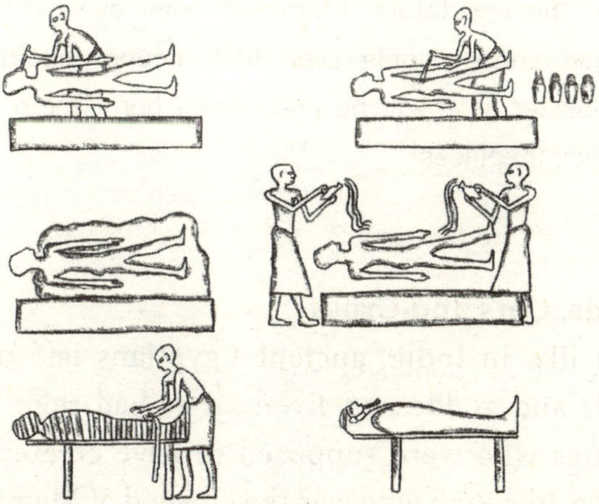

The mummification process

comes from! It has nothing to do with mothers. A mummy is very fragile and at times when the bandages were unwrapped, they just crumbled into dust. So nowadays the bandages are not removed, instead they are studied by a CAT scan and tiny scraps of skin are analyzed for DNA that can often identify who the dead person is.

A Great Show

In the 19th century hundreds of mummies were brought to England. A doctor named Pettigrew of the Royal College of Surgeons held a show where people could watch him unwrap a mummy. Tickets were sold and refreshments were served to the spectators. Mummies were everywhere and some people even had ground mummy powder as medicine and others burnt them in their fireplaces!

Gods, Cats and Crocs

Just like in India, ancient Egyptians had many gods and goddesses. Even cities had their own deities who were supposed to have created the place, like Ptah who was the city god of Memphis.

Among the most important was Ra, the sun god, who was also the father of many deities. Amun, who was the city god of Thebes, was his son and so he was called Amun Ra. His son was Shu, the god of air, and Shu had a daughter Nut, the sky goddess and a son, Geb the god of earth. Nut and Geb had two children—Osiris the god of the dead and Isis the mother goddess—and with Osiris and Isis the story of the pharaohs begins.

The story goes that the god Osiris was killed by his evil brother Seth and his body was cut into pieces but his sister-wife Isis found the pieces. With the help of Anubis, the jackal-headed god of the dead, she reassembled his body and Osiris came to life again. Isis and Osiris had a son called Horus who fought and killed Seth. Horus was

The gods of ancient Egypt

said to be the first king of Egypt. So the pharaohs all claimed to be the god Horus who had come down to earth and expected their subjects to worship them.

Many of the gods were imagined to have animal heads like the crocodile-headed Sobek, the god of water, and the goddess of childbirth Taweret, who had the face of a smiling hippopotamus. Horus's wife Hathor, the goddess of love and beauty, had the head of a cow. The mother goddess Bastet had the head of a cat and she was very popular because many pet cats were also mummified by her worshippers. The most magnificent was Sekhmet, a woman with the head of a lion who was the goddess of war.

Praying at Temples

The pharaohs built magnificent temples filled with pillared halls, the walls covered in carvings and paintings. They were all identical because the Egyptians believed that the first temple was designed by a god. Only the royal family and the priests and priestesses were allowed into temples. At the temples, the religious rituals were pretty similar to what we have in India. The image of the god would be brought out every day, bathed, dressed and then food would be offered to it. As the priests chanted prayers, the temple dancers

An ancient Egyptian temple

would sing sacred hymns and dance to entertain the god.

Most people would say their prayers at the shrines at home and when they wanted to pray to the deity at the temple they would pray before images placed at the gates. Here the scribes would wait for the pilgrims because when people had any special prayer, they would dictate their question or request to a scribe. The question could only be answered with a 'yes' or 'no' like—'Will I pass in maths?' or 'Will I get married this year?' The scribe would then take the question inside and come back with an answer claiming that it was a message from the god when it was really a reply from a priest.

So at popular temples, the priests and priestesses became very powerful as they claimed that they heard the words of the gods.

They were known as the oracles. The largest religious complex to have survived till today is at Karnak, near Luxor, and it has the ruins of many temples. Another complex of temples was found at Abu Simbel in Upper Egypt in 1817. While constructing the Aswan dam in the 1960s, a whole ancient temple here had to be shifted as it would have sunk below the waters of the dam's reservoir. In 1964, the temple was cut into blocks and shifted piece by piece to a higher ground over four years.

Where Is My Papyrus?

The word paper comes from the Egyptian word papyrus. They made one of the earliest papers in the world using a reed called papyrus that grew on the bank of the Nile. These reeds were also used to build boats. The sheets of papyrus were not easy to make and took quite a lot of time. They cut the reed into thin strips, soaked them in water, laid the strips in a criss-cross fashion, covered them with a cloth and pressed it with a stone to make it smooth and then dried

An ancient papyrus scroll

it. Papyrus was expensive and was only used to keep government records. For daily needs, scribes wrote on clay tablets like they did in Mesopotamia.

What script did the Egyptians use? Well, they had three! The first was a pictorial script used in carvings and paintings on walls in tombs called hieroglyphics, a Greek word meaning sacred carvings. It was a pretty script full of pictures like eyes and birds, walking men and squiggly lines but it took a lot of time to write. So the scribes developed two simpler scripts called hieratic and demotic that were used for daily work such as keeping records.

No one could read the hieroglyphics till 1799, when the soldiers of the French conqueror Napoleon's army found a stone at a place called Rosetta. On the stone the same message had been carved in three scripts: hieroglyphics, demotic and Greek. A Frenchman Jean Francois Champollion cracked the code in 1822 by using the familiar Greek words. Now we know that each picture stands for a sound and if you try hard enough you can write your name in hieroglyphics but it will sound a bit strange because the script did not have any vowels!

Going to School

Usually only the children of the rich went to school and among the important professions was that of a scribe, government official or engineer. Of course, it was not easy because you had to learn three scripts and the training to become a scribe lasted for twelve years. In school the subjects taught included mathematics, history, literature, religion, geography, and also technical subjects like surveying, engineering, astronomy, medicine and accounting. Students practised writing on pieces of broken pottery and a wax tablet that was a wooden board on which a layer of wax was applied. They wrote using a stylus and if they made a mistake, they just smoothed the wax back.

Scribes were respected members of society and as a scribe you could work keeping records in a royal office or collecting taxes at a temple; some scribes became teachers and librarians. Many scribes like Imhotep became powerful men by working with noblemen and the royal family as officials, and one of them, Horemheb, even became a pharaoh. As a scribe noted, 'Be a scribe so that you may be saved from being a soldier.'

A Maths Problem

A fragment of a papyrus was found with this maths problem written on it:

Problem: There are 7 houses. Each house has 7 cats. Each cat kills 7 mice. Each mouse ate 7 grains of barley. Each grain, if planted, would have produced 7 hekats of barley. Give the total number of houses, cats, mice and grain.

Answer: Houses – 7. Cats – 49. Mice – 343. Barley grains – 2401. Hekats of barley – 16807. So the grand total is – 19607. Pretty easy, actually!

Students and scribes are often shown with shaven heads except for a pigtail on one side, very like the ones worn by Brahmins in India. We can learn a lot about Egypt from the clay tablets kept by the scribes. For example, one scribe who kept records of the attendance of workers at a building site, also kept a list of the excuses given by workers for being late or taking a day off: illness; a fight with the wife; busy brewing beer for a festival; attending a funeral; a hangover after drinking too much beer; a child's birthday. The only excuse missing is—got stuck in a traffic jam.

Queens, Princesses and Slaves

We have to study the paintings and read the official records to discover the life of Egyptian women. What is clear from the paintings is that they moved around freely in society, there was no seclusion or veils. There are portraits of women all dressed up in fancy clothes and make-up, enjoying glasses of wine at parties. Other women are shown dancing and playing musical instruments to entertain guests at parties. There are terracotta models of maids carrying baskets and they are quite well-dressed, too, wearing jewellery and pretty clothes.

The records show that women could own property and they managed it themselves as there are records of them fighting legal cases and also running businesses and paying taxes. Divorce was allowed and the mother was given the custody of her children, and she could remarry. Among the powerful women were the queens and the priestesses in the temples. All the officials were men but often when their husbands were travelling or ill, the wives would take over their work. One odd profession reserved for women was of mourners who were hired when someone died. They would walk with the funeral procession weeping and wailing, throwing dust over their heads as if they were filled with grief when most of the time, they did not know the dead person at all!

Within the royal family the throne descended from the queen and often the king married a sister or half-sister. The senior wife always sat beside the pharaoh on the throne and was involved in the running of the kingdom. At times, when the pharaoh was too young, the mother would act as regent like Queen Nefertari. Another queen Nefertiti, the senior wife of Akhenaten, ruled beside her husband and is shown in paintings and carvings. The most famous was of course Hatshepsut who had the courage to rule as a pharaoh and even led the kingdom during war. Finally, there was Cleopatra VII, the last ruler of ancient Egypt who also ruled as an independent pharaoh and dealt with the Roman Empire.

I Am a Citizen

The cities in Egypt had narrow lanes with houses on both sides and the homes of the rich were built up to four storeys. The problem was that cities had no sewage or garbage disposal system and families had to bury the garbage in pits. So the lanes were pretty smelly and people spent a lot of time in the rooms on the upper floors and on summer nights, they slept on the roof. The rich had homes with gardens and many servants but the poor lived in small single-room houses.

Egyptian society was divided into many classes. Right at the top was the king who was the head of society and the royal family and they lived in the city. Below them were the upper classes of the nobility, ministers and priests. The middle classes had merchants, craftsmen, scribes and soldiers. Then came the farmers, servants and finally at the bottom were the slaves.

Both men and women used jewellery and make-up, especially around the eyes. They lined their eyes with kohl, lips and cheeks were coloured red and hands and feet painted with henna patterns. The rich also used perfume like myrrh, which was very expensive. When attending parties or any royal ceremonies people wore wigs that were hung with beads and jewels. Many paintings show bejewelled women dancing but never with men.

In the Villages

Most of the people lived in villages and it was the farms that made Egypt prosper. The bank of the Nile was lined with fields and villages nestled under palm trees. They grew wheat for bread and barley for beer, flax for linen, dates, grapes and a wide variety of vegetables.

There were also villages of craftsmen as they worked at building sites of temples and tombs. At the Valley of Kings, the work on the tombs went on for centuries and a village of craftsmen grew there. This was excavated at a place called Deir el Medinah and it revealed well-off people who had large homes and some of them had even built their own tombs. The working week for the craftsmen was eight days of work, then two days off and holidays on sixty-five holy days. Wages were paid in kind with food, oil, linen, firewood and often a bonus of salt, wine, meat and silver. In the records we also find that the workers went on strike when their wages were late. Unlike what people believed, the pharaohs did not use slaves but trained craftspeople and farmers.

Invitation to a Feast

The rich often threw lavish banquets where a wide variety of dishes and wines were served. Guests were welcomed with flower garlands and served exotic dishes like roast goose, fish and meats, cakes, figs and desserts sweetened with honey. Musicians played flutes, pipes and drums as singers, dancers, acrobats and jugglers entertained the guests. People are always shown wearing white clothes. The grandest were the dresses worn by the queens that were finely pleated and at times so delicate they were nearly transparent. Make-up boxes have been found with the black kohl, green eye shadow and henna, which was used to redden the lips and fingers.

Both men and women wore jewellery, especially the typical Egyptian collar of beads and precious stones. One strange custom was that when guests arrived, they were handed a cone of perfumed wax that they placed on their heads. The heat melted the wax and kept their heads cool. Luckily most of them wore wigs, so their hair wasn't ruined. If you look carefully at the Egyptian paintings, you'll see the cones on top of the heads of the guests.

Egypt Goes Greek

The pharaohs were conquered by the Persians in 525 BCE and then in 332 BCE the Greek conqueror Alexander defeated the Persians and made Egypt a part of his empire. The Egyptians hated the Persians and welcomed Alexander as a saviour. As a matter of fact, the oracle at a temple even said that he was the son of the god Amun Ra. When he died nine years later, his empire that stretched from Greece to India, was divided among his generals and Egypt fell in the share of his cousin Ptolemy. In 305 BCE, Ptolemy I proclaimed himself the pharaoh and founded the Ptolemaic dynasty that lasted till 31 BCE.

During this time all the important posts were held by Greeks and the pharaoh Ptolemy XIII married a sister or stepsister Cleopatra and they ruled together. The Greeks had a tradition of writing down their history so the Greek pharaohs got the history of their reigns recorded. The Greek historian Herodotus visited Egypt, and Ptolemy II got the Egyptian scribe Manetho to write the history. It was he who divided the history into thirty dynasties.

Alexander had founded a new city named Alexandria by the shores of the Mediterranean. Ptolemy I made it his capital and Alexander's embalmed body was kept here. The port became a centre of art and culture and had a museum and a famous library. The Ptolemaic dynasty remained Greek, marrying within the family and speaking Greek. However, they respected Egyptian traditions and even wore the royal headdress and worshipped the Egyptian gods and goddesses.

Cleopatra VII, the last ruler of the dynasty, ruled as a pharaoh even though she was pure Greek. At that time, the Roman Empire was rising and in an attempt to save her kingdom she first allied with the Roman ruler Julius Caesar and when he was assassinated, she married the general Mark Anthony. However, when she and Anthony were defeated, they both committed suicide, Anthony by a sword and she let herself be bitten by a poisonous snake called asp. Thus the dynasty of Greek pharaohs came to an end and Egypt became a part of the Roman Empire.

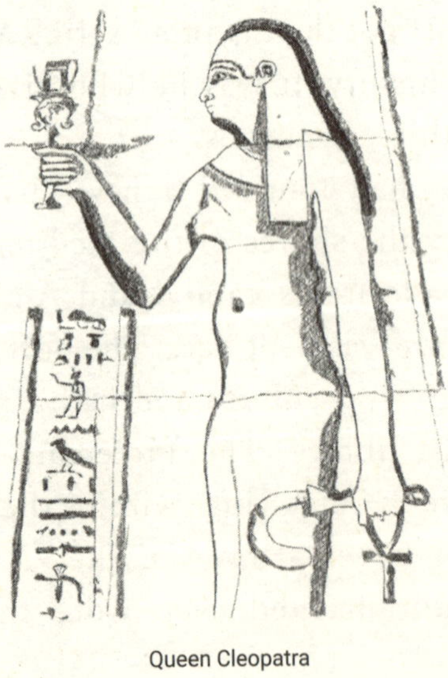

Queen Cleopatra

As a Roman colony, it converted to Christianity during the reign of Constantine and the old religion of gods and goddesses died out. Then it was conquered by Muslim rulers and became an Islamic nation, even though it still has a Christian population called Copts. In today's Egypt no one prays to Osiris or Horus anymore.

EXCITING EGYPT

- Among the divine symbols of the royal family were the falcon, bees and the pillars called obelisks. Beards were considered divine and both male and female pharaohs wore false beards.
- Khufu, the pharaoh who built the great pyramid at Giza, was for some strange reason called Cheops by the Greeks, adding to the confusion.
- The bust of Queen Nefertiti, wife of Pharaoh Akhenaten, is the most famous Egyptian profile in the world. Her name translates as 'A Beautiful One Has Come'.
- One of the men who excavated many tombs was an eccentric Englishman named William Flinders Petrie. As Egypt is a hot country he often worked wearing long, bright pink underwear.

- When the mummy of Ramesses II was taken to France for an exhibition, it got its own French passport. Here it was discovered that the mummy had been attacked by beetles and scientists were called to treat it.
- The Egyptians played a board game called Senet that had a board in the shape of a cross, with dice and markers. One set was found intact inside the tomb of Tutankhamun. It looks similar to the Indian board game called pachisi.
- The Egyptians made forty different kinds of bread, both sweet and salty. They also brewed beer from barley and wine from grapes.
- Today camels are synonymous with Egypt but during the ancient times they only used donkeys. Camels were introduced by the Arab traders.
- The Mayans and Aztecs of Mexico also built pyramids between the 13th and 15th centuries CE but these were not tombs. There was a temple on top dedicated to the sun god. The Mexicans had never heard of Egypt.
- After the French conqueror Napoleon Bonaparte conquered Egypt, he spent some time alone inside the burial chamber of Khufu's pyramid and came out looking quite shaken. He never told anyone what he experienced there.

- The Egyptians were the first to create a calendar year of 365 days with twelve months of thirty days and five extra days at the end.
- In 1997, at a place called Bawati, a donkey tripped over hole in the ground. Digging there, archaeologists found a huge tomb with hundreds of mummies.
- Hieroglyphics can be read left to right, right to left and top to bottom. You check which way the birds are facing because they always face the beginning of the sentence.
- The Rosetta Stone was found by the French but the English took it away when they defeated Napoleon. Today you can see it at the British Museum in London.
- During the reign of the Greeks, Alexandria had a giant lighthouse called Pharos that was one of the seven wonders of the ancient world.
- The Americans built a city they named Memphis after the Egyptian city and the singer Elvis Presley lived there.
- Egypt often inspires books and films. The British Museum's acquisition of the statue of Ramesses II, inspired the poet Percy Shelley to compose the poem 'Ozymandias'.

The Indus Valley

A Mysterious People

(2600 BCE–1300 BCE)

In the 19th century, English travellers noticed some mysterious piles of mud bricks in the desert areas of Sind, which was then in north India (and now in Pakistan). The bricks looked very old but the local people had no idea what they were for or who made them. All they could say was that for generations they had helped themselves to these readymade bricks, to build their homes. As the bricks covered a large area, they must have been used to build a town but who were these people who made such a large city and why did they go away? Even people with the wildest imagination could not have guessed that the bricks holding up a farmer's thatched hut were over 4000 years old.

As it has been revealed through nearly a century of excavations, these were the remains of the world's first planned cities with the first

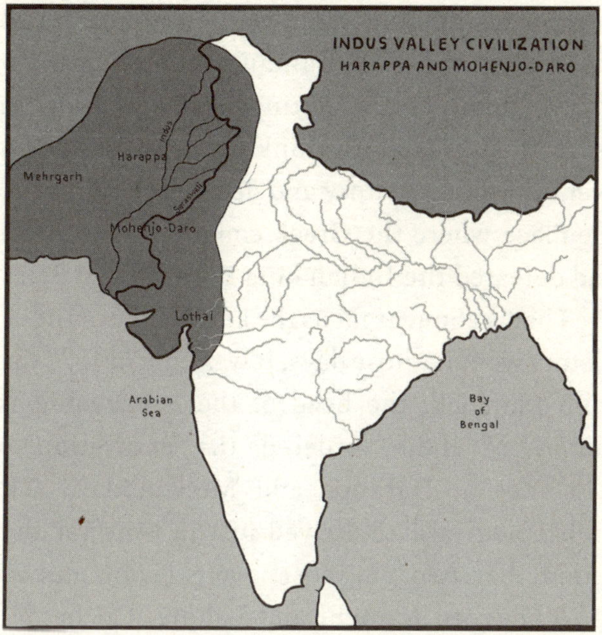

proper drainage systems. It was a civilization that flourished at the same time as Mesopotamia and Egypt, but had been forgotten for a long long time. It was the Indus Valley Civilization.

So Many Bricks!

In 1826 Charles Masson, a soldier of the East India Company, stood on a mysterious earthen mound near a village called Harappa in the Punjab, looked around a strange landscape and felt there was something unique about the place and wrote of exploring, 'a ruinous brick castle having remarkable high walls and towers'. It looked like the site of an ancient settlement or even a famous battle. Letting his imagination run wild, Masson tried to think of the most ancient event in India's history and decided that this was the place where the Greek conqueror Alexander had defeated the Indian king Porus in 326 BCE.

That is about as far as the knowledge of India's history went in those days. It was only in 1872 that John Marshall, the head of the Archaeological Survey of India, ordered the excavation of two sites at Harappa and Mohenjodaro. The archaeologists had arrived just in time for they found that two engineers were laying railway lines between Karachi and Lahore and happily taking away cartloads of the 4000-year-old bricks to use in their tracks. Luckily, they were stopped from turning Harappa into a railway platform and the remains of India's first civilization was saved.

The two biggest cities of the Indus Valley Civilization are Mohenjodaro that once stood on the bank of the River Indus, 320 kilometres from Karachi; and Harappa, built on the bank of the River Ravi, 160 kilometres from Lahore—both now in Pakistan. The rivers have moved away and today Harappa is 10 kilometres from the Ravi and Mohenjodaro, 5 kilometres from the Indus. When the excavations began, whole cities were discovered with roads, buildings, water tanks and drainage systems. Also, as you can see in the gallery at the National Museum in Delhi, there were pottery, terracotta images, toys, jewellery, and many seals with images and a puzzling writing on them that no one can read.

The story of the Indus people is like a historical jigsaw puzzle with many of the pieces still missing. The writing on the seals is the key to our finding out more but sadly even computers have failed to decipher what was written. So a lot of history is a kind of guesswork with historians imagining a people, their lives, religion, political system only from what has been revealed during the excavations. With the discovery of these

The ruins at Harappa

cities, suddenly India's history was moved back by over 2000 years and it was counted among the oldest civilizations in the world. The Indus River and its tributaries, Ravi, Sutlej and Ghaggar, gave birth to the first cities in India.

The Harappan Timeline

With modern science and a process called radiocarbon dating of the material found during excavations, three distinct phases of the Harappan Civilizations have been marked:

Early Harappan—3200-2600 BCE

Mature Harappan—2600–1900 BCE

Late Harappan—1900–1300 BCE

The Mature Harappan period is when the great cities were flourishing. The late Harappan period saw the decline of the cities and the gradual shifting of the population that abandoned the cities.

Historians Turn Detectives

Archaeologists are like detectives looking for clues in what they dig up. They can date a piece of pottery from the layer in the excavations and they study bones and remains of grains in a pot to tell us what people ate at that time. A sculpture will tell us what people wore and a weapon how they fought battles. It is slow, painstaking work: carefully digging into a mound, meticulously listing and preserving everything they find and slowly building up an image of the people who had lived there.

Among the first archaeologists who worked at the Harappan sites were the Indians Rakhal Das Banerji, Daya Ram Sahni and Madho Sarup Vats along with Englishmen John Marshall and Mortimer Wheeler. Banerji and Sahni laboured away in the burning hot sun of summers slowly and carefully revealing a city street by street, house by house. In the following decades many more sites were found. If you plot the total of 1022 sites on a world map, you will see that 406 of the sites are in Pakistan and 616 are in India. These sites spread from western Uttar Pradesh to Haryana, Jammu, Rajasthan and Gujarat; then across the border in Punjab, Sind, the North-West Frontier and Baluchistan. The largest cities of Mohenjodaro and Harappa are in Pakistan. The cities in India are Kalibangan (Rajasthan), Rupar (Punjab), Rakhigarhi (Haryana), Lothal and Dholavira (Gujarat).

Copycat Cities

The local people call the ruins Mohenjodaro, or the Mound of the Dead but in fact no one knows the original name. Archaeologists think the cities were built around 2600 BCE, the same time as the Mesopotamian civilization. By 1500 BCE, the cities had been abandoned and were soon in ruins as rows and rows of mud-brick houses slowly crumbled in the harsh desert sun. Miraculously they did not vanish, waiting stubbornly to be discovered again so that a forgotten people could tell us their stories.

What is astonishing is that the cities were all built in exactly the same manner. Looking at our chaotic, badly planned cities, it is hard to believe

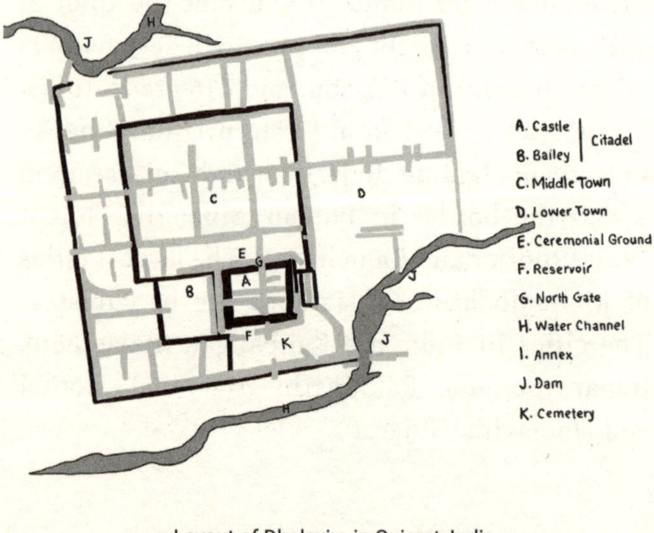

Layout of Dholavira in Gujarat, India

that we once had such well-planned cities! First, all the streets were laid out in straight lines as if the engineers were using geometry sets. These were the main avenues from which lanes led off and the houses are in these lanes. Interestingly, at the crossings of the main avenues there were single rooms like police check-posts. You can easily imagine a policeman in a dhoti and a pugree sitting there, waving his lathi and yelling at bullock-cart drivers who did not obey the traffic rules.

Up to 40,000 people could have lived in Mohenjodaro, the largest city. The cities were divided into localities and a raised area called a citadel stood on a high earthen platform surrounded by a wall. It must have been where the government offices and the homes of the ruling elite stood. The remains of wheat, barley and the husks of grain found here indicate that the citadel also had the granaries where the grains given by the farmers as taxes were stored. All the cities had villages around them that supplied the food and provided the labour for construction work. Polluting industries like brick kilns and the potters were all located outside the city walls.

What is amazing is that cities hundreds of kilometres apart are all made of brick in exactly the same way! The bricks are 7x14x28 cm for homes and 10x20x40 cm for city walls as if they were all from one single factory. Also, unlike our modern cities, where nothing is maintained well, the city walls at Harappa were constantly repaired and strengthened. So they must have had hundreds of city planners, engineers and supervisors at work and a very efficient administration. The main streets are 10 metres wide, so there must have been quite a heavy traffic of people, bullock carts and maybe palanquins and elephants.

How did they plan and build identical cities 4000 years ago? After all, they could not email a design to an architect or phone instructions to the man making the bricks. All the houses have the same plan with a single door opening into a side lane. All rooms in the houses are built around an open courtyard, and the windows open into it. Some houses have a second floor and the residents may have slept on the roofs in summer like we do even today. Most of the houses had a bathing area and a toilet with drains leading to the main sewers. The cities were neat and precisely planned but also kind of grim as there were no decorations. We are used to cities that are a constant panorama of vivid, ever changing colours and shapes. Here, everything was kept regimented like army barracks. No one built a luxurious house or added pretty carvings on the walls or windows.

Let's Talk of Drains

A drainage system is not very romantic but can any city survive without garbage collection and sewers? The Indus people clearly took cleanliness very, very seriously. Modern city planners have been amazed at the wonderfully planned underground drainage system. The water from homes flowed into sewers through terracotta pipes to the river and these pipes were so well made that they have survived till today. These cities were the cleanest in the world!

The Harappans clearly liked bathing a lot—there were homes with bathrooms, large pools, wells and then of course there was the river itself. They bathed the way Indians do even today, using a bucket of water and a mug made of environment-friendly terracotta (not plastic). The drainage pipes had manhole covers so the pipes could be cleaned and garbage was collected from the homes and thrown outside the city boundaries. So we know that the cities had efficiently run municipality departments. Sadly, in the centuries that followed, Indians forgot how to build an underground drainage system and even a hundred years ago many small towns had open, stinking drains.

Trading Across the Seas

Lothal, one of the Indus cities in Gujarat, stood by the Arabian Sea and was a port from where goods from the Indus cities were sent to the Persian Gulf. There is a patch of water with a wall around it that looks like a dockyard and there is a sluice gate and a spill channel to control the level of water. On the bank is a wharf where the goods were loaded and unloaded from ships and stone anchors have been found, proving ships docked here. Lothal, like all ports, must have been a lively place with sailors from strange lands wandering around its busy streets.

There was an overland trade route going through Afghanistan and Persia and caravans travelled to Mesopotamia. At Akkad, records from the time of the reign of King Sargon (2334–2279 BCE) mention three lands that the Sumerian people traded with. These are called Dilmun, Magan and Meluhha. Historians think Dilmun was Bahrain, Magan was Oman and Meluhha was probably Mohenjodaro. The Indus cities traded in jewellery, pottery and also cotton which was always India's biggest export, right till the time of the British. The historian A.L.

Basham feels that cotton cloth was probably first woven in India and fragments of ancient Indian textiles have been found in many parts of Asia. If you study the patterns woven and printed on them, they look pretty similar to the saris and skirts that we wear today.

Address: Mohenjodaro

What was it like to live in these cities? What did they have for lunch? Did children play with toys? Did they worship gods and goddesses?

From food items found in pots and jars we know they ate wheat, barley, pulses, watermelon, peas, dates, rice, millet, grapes, horse gram, chickpea, sesame seed and garlic. So a breakfast of barley porridge and fried chickpeas sounds pretty appetising. Also, they ate many kinds of pulses like masoor and moong dal and the food must have been cooked in sesame or linseed oil. Maybe they also brewed wine from grapes and beer from barley like they did in Mesopotamia. Archaeologists even uncovered a field that was ploughed in neat rows for planting a crop exactly like farmers do today.

The bones of many animals—like deer, pigs, goat, boar, sheep, tortoise, fish, and most surprisingly the gharial, the snout-nosed river crocodile—have been found. People must have made meat curries or fried some fish to go with the wheat rotis but how did they catch and cook a gharial? How does crocodile meat taste? The imagination boggles a bit. In the kitchens, grinding stones have been found, used to grind wheat and masala. Also metal and clay tawas like the ones we use to make rotis and parathas. The food was cooked on chulas made of earth using wood as fuel. One copper pan with a long handle looks exactly like the pans we use to fry omelettes.

People wore two unstitched lengths of cotton like we still do with the sari, dhoti and lungi. One length was knotted at the waist and another wrapped around the upper body, under the right arm and then over the left shoulder. Bone needles show they wore stitched blouses but none of the sculptures or seals show people wearing fancy clothes. But when it came to hairstyles and jewellery, they were trendy and fashionable. One fashion, as seen on the image of the Dancing Girl and the horned male figure on a seal, is the left arm being covered with

bangles right from the wrist to the upper arm and necklaces with pendants. The hair was twisted and tied in elaborate hairdos—long plaits, knots at the top of the head or at the neck and two circlets shaped like doughnuts above the ears like Princess Leia in *Star Wars*. Archaeologists have found bronze mirrors, razors and boxes with dried colours that could be make-up kits. The colours include black kohl used to line the eyes; red henna to paint the hand, feet and lips; white and green paint maybe for some quick skin whitening and green eye shadow.

The clay toys are balls, rattles, whistles and even a funny monkey that runs up and down a stick. Indians have always enjoyed board games and one day we would invent chess. Square dice and playing pieces have been found but no boards because they must have been made of wood. The toys and drawings on pottery also give us an idea of the way they travelled. There are bullock carts with a covered top and two heavy wheels and also drawings of boats with sails.

A terracota bullock cart

A Citadel and a Great Bath

The city was divided into the main settlement and the citadel that was built on a high platform and protected by a thick wall. We can only guess at the purpose of the buildings but it does feel like they were the centre of power. The buildings have been given names such as the tower, the granary, a college for priests and a bath but once again it

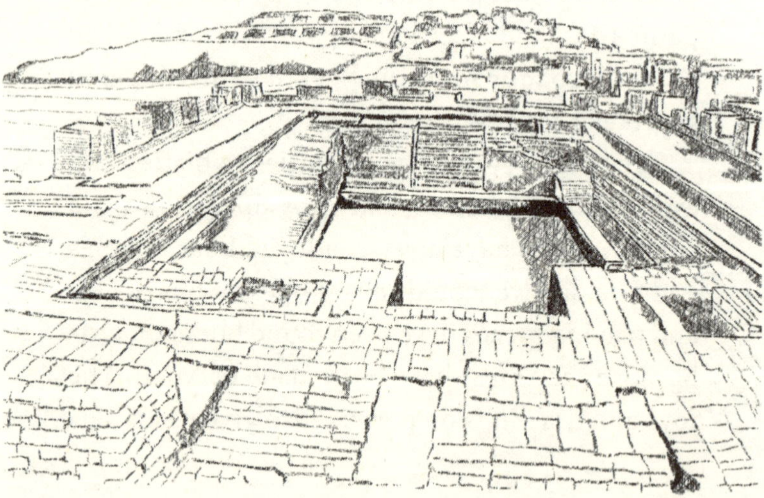

The Great Bath at Mohenjodaro

The town with its citadel, the centre of power

is all guesswork. In the citadel in Mohenjodaro, there is a large pool called the Great Bath, very similar to water tanks that we have at temples. It is 14.5 by 7 metres with a depth of 2.4 metres and has steps on two sides leading to the water.

In those days they did not have cement, then how did they make the pool watertight? The bricks were fitted very closely and then a layer of tar was poured over it. The floor was sloped to an outlet to drain the water like we have in swimming pools. Most houses had bathing areas, lanes had wells in corners and there was also the river, so this may not have been a public swimming pool. It must have served some religious ritual like people bathing before entering a temple to worship.

Potters, Jewellers and Brick Makers

Many kinds of pottery have been found—pots, pans, plates, bowls and large storage jars for grain and oil. They were all made on the potter's wheel and then fired in a kiln and in the same designs. Many pots are in a lovely deep maroon colour with black designs painted on them. The designs are simple: flowers, leaves, geometric

patterns, animals and fish, similar to the earthenware we see in our bazaars.

The making of bead necklaces was a big industry as many workshops have been found with half-finished beads lying around. The shaping, drilling and polishing required quite a lot of expertise and they were made of semi-precious stones like carnelian, agate, amethyst, crystal and lapis lazuli. The designs are so pretty you could use them in a fashion show today. Imagine models sashaying down the catwalk with Harappan bead necklaces swaying around their thin necks.

The jewellery was highly valued in other countries and some of these items were found in many tombs in Mesopotamia. The most interesting crafts site is Kalibangan in Rajasthan, which was

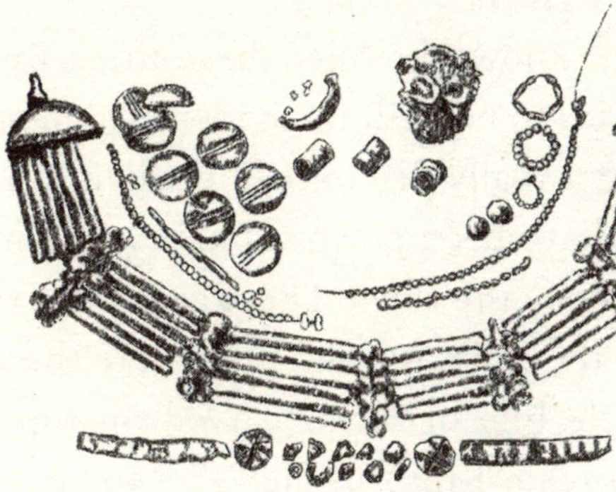

a bangle factory. Kalibangan means black bangle and archaeologists found hundreds of bangles in black terracotta and of shell, alabaster, soapstone and copper. They also discovered elegant ivory combs that would look very pretty sticking out of a hairdo. The materials used in the jewellery were brought from far-off places. The conch shell came from Kathiawar in Gujarat and the Deccan; silver, turquoise and lapis lazuli from Persia and Afghanistan; copper from Rajasthan and the jadeite from as far away as Tibet and Central Asia. The trade routes on land and sea must have been quite busy and we can imagine traders travelling long distances to supply the jewellers of the Indus cities and then taking their creations to the markets of Ur and Akkad.

Kings and Priests

We still don't know who ruled these cities. But for so many cities to be built in an identical manner, it had to be a really disciplined civilization and there must have been powerful kings who made the people obey the rules. There are no carvings that record their history; all we have are the seals with a single line of script carved on top that no one can read. Kings usually like to show off and build temples, forts, palaces and then get buried in elaborate tombs. However here there are no temples like the Mesopotamian zigurrats, no tombs like the Egyptian pyramids, no royal graves filled with treasures. Some historians speculate that priests ruled the cities.

The citadels may have been where the ruling elite lived and some of the buildings were temples. The reason no religious images have been found could be because this region did not have stone and images were made of wood that did not survive. The way the cities are planned and built does show that there was an efficient administration with officers going around scratching their chin as they measured the width of streets, supervised the building of the drainage system and checked the size of the bricks to make sure that they were all identical.

What was created was a comfortable and well-run lifestyle but it was also rather colourless. We don't find the tombs with painted walls covered in dazzling paintings or giant stone carvings of gods, goddesses and pharaohs. There is none of the vivid pageantry of magnificent temples or majestic images. It is all properly organized, business-like and predictable. But the cities were planned keeping the people in mind. They were well built, well run and very comfortable to live in. Most ordinary people, even today, would prefer a good sewer system and efficient garbage collection to a fancy palace.

A Grim Man and a Dancing Girl

A few sculptures of human figures have been found, some headless, others in fragments. Among them is the sculpture of a very solemn man wearing some kind of a robe with a flower pattern with one end thrown across the left shoulder. His hair is parted in the middle and he has a decorated band tied across his forehead. His beard is neatly combed, his upper lip shaven and he stares back at you with heavy-lidded eyes looking a bit

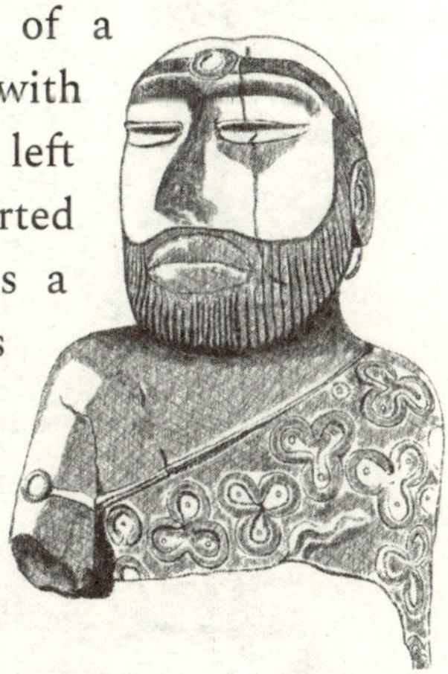

disapproving. His calm, unsmiling expression makes one think he may have been a ruler or a high priest as he is a bit grim and scary.

In contrast, the tiny female bronze figurine called the Dancing Girl makes you smile. Seeing her in the National Museum in Delhi, one is surprised at how small the image is and still so powerful. It was found in a house in Mohenjodaro in 1926 and John Marshall, who clearly found her delightful, named her the Dancing Girl. It was because of the way she is standing—the left leg bent at the knee as if she is tapping her feet to music, with her head tilted back and a slightly challenging smile on her face that says, 'Come and dance with me!'

The Dancing Girl is tiny, barely 11 centimetres high but she has so much personality! She looks barely out of her teens with a slim body and her hair is tied into a loose bun at her neck. Her arms are very long, the right one rests at her waist and the other on a bent knee and all she is wearing are a necklace and bangles, lots of them, and no clothes. Her left

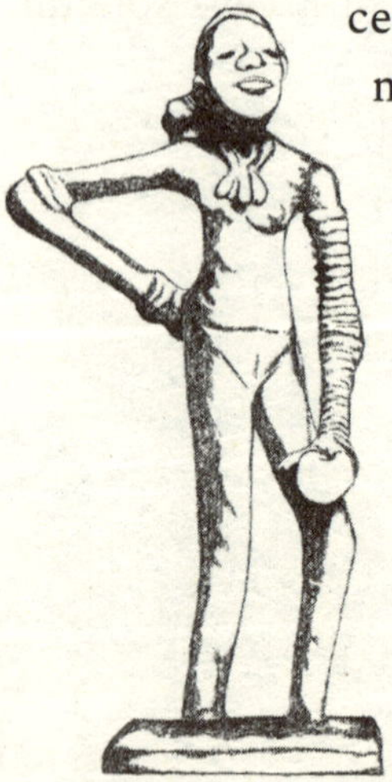

arm is covered in bangles from the wrist to the shoulder, very like the white bangles that women wear in Rajasthan.

Mysterious Seals

Among all the things they dug up, the most mysterious are the seals. Some say they were used to stamp on clay tablets but unlike Mesopotamia no tablet has been found. Others think they were used to mark packages of goods and some think they were identity cards that were worn around the neck by officials. It is all just wild guesswork and no one really knows. The seals have been found in Iraq, Iran, Afghanistan and Central Asia. Most are the size of a large postage stamp, made of a soft stone called steatite or soapstone. On one side there is a carving, usually of an animal—a bull, a rhinoceros, a tiger, a deer or a fish—and at times a human figure. It is hard to imagine rhinos wandering around the region today where only camels can be seen but these seals prove that at one time this land must have been covered with forests. The most impressive is the image of a majestic bull carved in profile with many dewlaps and a rhinoceros with its layered hide.

On the top half of the seal are carved what look like words in a pictorial script. Over 3700

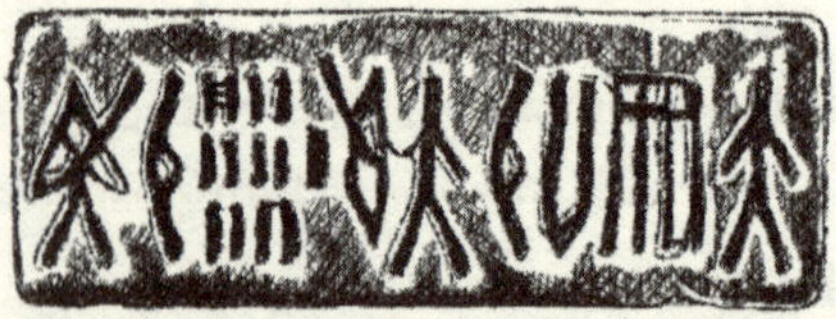

seals have been collected so far and nearly 80 per cent were found in Mohenjodaro and Harappa. Over 400 separate signs have been listed and historians think the script is pictorial—each sign stands for a word. They wrote from right to left and we can make that out because sometimes they ran out of space and squeezed in a sign at the end, like we do while doing our class work.

How Did They Pray?

Many clay figures have been found of women wearing huge fan-shaped headdresses. These could be images of goddesses. The women in these images wear a lot of jewellery, a short skirt and their hairdos are all quite elaborate. The images are roughly made and as they were often found inside homes they were probably worshipped as family icons. Some of the images even have the mark of fire like what happens when we put an incense stick next to an idol for long periods of time.

A goddess's idol

Another god-like image is of a thin man shown on some seals, though no terracotta image has been found. The majestic figure sits cross-legged in a yogic posture with his arms resting on his knees as if he is meditating. He wears a tall, horned headdress very similar to the ones that tribal dancers wear decorated with shells and feathers. Just like the Dancing Girl, he wears bangles and a short necklace. The cross-legged man seems to have three heads and is surrounded by four animals—a buffalo, an elephant, a rhinoceros, a tiger—and below his seat there are two deer. Some historians think it is an early form of the Hindu god Shiva because one of his forms was as Pashupati or the lord of animals. Maybe, maybe not... we can't be sure because we still can't read what the words on top of his head say.

The Cities Begin to Die

Historians wonder why around 1500 BCE, the cities were abandoned. This decline went on for many centuries as people gradually moved eastward and also towards the south. There are many theories about it but no one really knows what happened.

One theory is that there was some kind of an environmental disaster: the shifting of rivers, floods, drought or deforestation. The seals show animals like elephants and rhinoceros, so the area must have been very green and deeply forested unlike today when Sind, western Punjab and Rajasthan are a barren desert. Maybe this is the first example of the effect of deforestation because trees were cut for agriculture and used in firing the millions of bricks. At this time, the water levels of the Arabian Sea rose and the salty seawater flooding the land would have ruined it and made it impossible to grow crops.

The rivers may have shifted due to earthquakes and led to the drying up of the Ghaggar River as the Yamuna stopped flowing into it. The Indus changed its course because Mohenjodaro shows signs of flooding that covered the lower areas of the city.

The Indus people may have faced economic ruin because their biggest trade was with the cities of Mesopotamia and at this time the kingdoms of Sumer and Akkad were conquered by invaders. So the trade in cotton, pottery and jewellery that kept the city economy going may have ended. As excavations show, many of the villages survived much longer, so people may have left the cities and gone back to agriculture.

Here Come the Aryans

The next people who left a mark on Indian history are the Aryans who were nomadic cattle herders. These tribes were always on the move in search of grasslands for their sheep and cows. They began to move out of the steppes of Central Asia around the Caspian Sea probably because of extended drought. Some of the tribes migrated westward towards Europe and others moved eastward to Persia and Afghanistan and then into India. These waves of migration came at a time when the Indus cities were dying. The

Aryans spread slowly across north India as the Indus people moved southwards into the Deccan peninsula and became the ancestors of the Dravidian people.

We know about the Aryans because of their oldest book of prayers, the Rig Veda. The Rig Veda and the three more Vedas that followed have survived through the centuries because the verses were memorized and handed down through generations. The Rig Veda describes a life very different from those we find in the Indus cities. The nomadic Aryans did not build cities and what is puzzling is that they did not occupy the cities that were already there. Instead, the Rig Veda shows a dislike of city people, calling them dark-skinned and 'dasas' or slaves and poems of praise describe cities being burnt by their god Indra. They worshipped gods that are similar to the gods of ancient Persia like Indra, Varuna and Agni. Unlike the Indus Valley, they had no script and did not build using bricks and their temporary settlements of thatched huts vanished a long time ago.

Recently some historians have claimed that the Aryans were the original people of India and that the Indus Valley Civilization was in fact an Aryan one. However, there is no archaeological proof that the Aryans built the cities because if they had, then the Vedas would certainly have mentioned it. Also, the Indus Valley and the Aryan civilizations have nothing in common. The Aryans share both a language and a pantheon of deities with the people of Persia and Europe and this language can be traced back to the tribes of Central Asia. The Indus people worshipped goddesses while the early Aryans did not and even Shiva became an Aryan god much later.

The Aryans were a warlike people, proud of their martial prowess, often talking of battles and all their gods had their favourite weapons while the Indus people were a peaceful community and were mainly craftsmen and traders. The Aryans had tamed the horse and used it in battle while the

Mass graves discovered during excavations

Indus people did not, as no seal shows a horse or a chariot. The poems in the Rig Veda talk about the god Indra fighting battles and using many kinds of weapons. In the Indus Valley cities, no swords, shields or armour have been found, and even the few spears and axes excavated were badly made in bronze and must have been used for hunting, not battle.

There was no planned Aryan invasion but waves of migration by various Aryan tribes who gradually replaced the people in the cities. There must have been some conflict as on the top-most layer of excavations, skeletons have been found lying on streets and in homes as if killed by invaders. As they moved eastward, the Aryans gradually abandoned their pastoral life and began to live in villages. But it would be a thousand years before new cities were built by the banks of the Ganga River and they were vastly different from the Indus Valley cities.

HELLO HARAPPA!

- The streets of the Indus Valley cities are laid down in straight lines and at right angles, just like New York. To plan cities with such precision the architects and city planners must have known both arithmetic and geometry.

- Unlike all other civilizations, there is no display of spectacular wealth. No palaces, tombs, temples, hoards of jewellery or gold. It is remarkable that the leaders, who may have been kings or priests, chose to live so simply.
- The Great Bath is the first example of waterproofing in the world. While the Egyptians used tar to preserve the mummies, the practical people of Harappa preferred a nice swimming pool.
- Among the many kinds of pottery there are these tall jars with perforations that were found in the kitchens. What did the cooks need them for?
- No weapons like swords or shields, armour or helmets have been found.
- They did not know the use of iron but used copper or bronze.
- No seal has a horse carved on it and strangely they only have bulls but not cows.
- Bits of woven cotton cloth and spinning wheels have been found here and some historians think the weaving of cotton cloth may have begun in India.

- A buried hoard of nearly 500 pieces of jewellery was found in Harappa in a poor locality. Could it have been the hidden stash of a thief?
- At the ruins of a brick kiln, you can still see the footmarks of a cat being chased by a dog that got imprinted on the wet clay bricks laid out to dry in the sun.

China

Inventions and Creativity (2200 BCE–220 CE)

China is a land with high mountain ranges and huge sandy deserts in the north and the Indian Ocean in the south. This forbidding landscape isolated the Chinese from the rest of the world and hence they developed their own unique civilization. It is a huge country, not just bigger than India, but also the United States. They have many races but the majority of the people belong to the ancient tribe called Han and it is their language and culture that holds the Chinese people together.

Like in all ancient civilizations, the first human settlements were around its three big rivers: the Huang He, Yangtze and Xi Jiang and their network of tributaries. Agriculture began in China around 9000 BCE with the cultivation of grains like millet. Later the farmers learnt to grow rice and that helped the population to

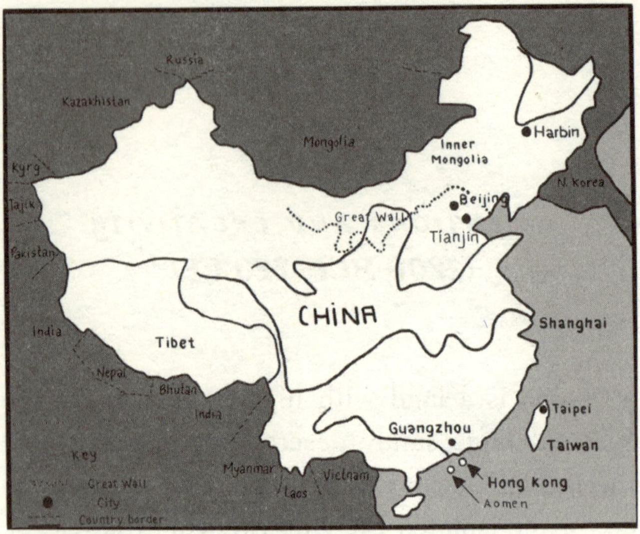

grow rapidly and led to the foundation of cities. China was ruled by a series of dynasties from 221 BCE to 1912 CE, making it the oldest and longest empire in the world.

The Han tribe settled in the fertile lands around the Huang He or the Yellow River about 12,000 years ago. In the beginning, they were hunters and fishermen but gradually they began growing food, keeping cattle and then making pottery. By 1500 BCE, they were making bronze items, weaving silk and had developed a pictorial form of writing. What is much more interesting is that they soon began to eat noodles made from rice powder; and instead of using spoons they were eating them using two sticks we call chopsticks and steaming up delicious plates of dim sum!

So Many Kings!

Now, if a civilization is so old it will also have many kings, priesthood and a bureaucracy. As the Chinese made weapons and began riding horses and chariots, the men went off to conquer land. Later, the most powerful general became the king and China has had many dynasties over the years. The historians of ancient China mention dynasties going back to a time with no written records. The first dynasty in the 17th century BCE is called Xia but modern historians think these kings were mythical as they have found no evidence of their rule. It was followed by the Shang, Zhou, Qin and Han dynasties. The ones in modern times include the Yuan, Ming and the Manchu dynasties. The last Manchu king was deposed by the Communists in 1912 CE.

It was a king of the Qin dynasty who united all of China under one ruler in 221 BCE, creating a kingdom. He is called Shi Huang Di or the 'First Emperor'. He was a great warrior but also a tyrant who ruled by strict laws and harsh punishment. He was a very efficient king. He created a system of administration, built roads and irrigation

Qin Shi Huang Di

canals that united the country. All of China had the same kinds of weights and measures as well as coins, and the fussy king even decided on the exact circumference of wagon wheels!

The First Emperor did not like scholars who were often critical of his actions and in 212 BCE he burnt all books, even the works of the philosopher Confucius, and put 400 scholars to death because he thought they were not obedient. The only books he allowed to be written dealt with practical subjects like agriculture and medicine.

Chinese Dynasties

The following dynasties have reigned in China over the years: Xia (2205–1766 BCE), Shang (1766–1122 BCE), Zhou (1122–256 BCE), Qin

(221–206 BCE), Han (202 BCE–220 CE), Sui (589–618 CE), Tang (619–906 CE), Song (960–1279 CE), Yuan (1280–1367), Ming (1368–1643 CE), Manchu (1644–1912 CE).

One of the greatest dynasties was of the Ming who built the city of Beijing in the 13th century. There was the outer city where the common people lived and the inner city where the nobility had their mansions. These two cities were connected by the Tiananmen or the Gate of Heavenly Peace. Right at the centre of the inner city was the Forbidden City with many palaces all built for one man—the Ming Emperor and his household. Most Chinese never entered the Forbidden City or saw their emperor.

The Terracotta Warriors

Like the Egyptians, the Chinese also believed in life after death. So the grave chambers of kings were filled with all the things they might need after death, like furniture, food, clothes and jewellery. And the tough old 'First Emperor' Shi Huang Di, who was a bit different from most kings, decided he would go on fighting battles in heaven and thus needed an army of soldiers around his tomb.

In 1974, farmers digging a well in a field in Xian, in north central China, discovered a full-size human figure of a soldier made of terracotta. Archaeologists came rushing and began excavations and gradually unearthed over 7000 full-sized human figures of soldiers. It was an amazing sight: row after row of clay warriors, still standing in battle formation, carrying weapons and all guarding the royal tomb! There were also terracotta horses and chariots for this ghostly army. Some of the warriors are in armour and some have real weapons. What is amazing is that the faces are not identical. They were modelled on real people and all look different and are moulded in different poses: standing, crouching and sitting.

The bust of a clay warrior

A Very Long Wall

We all know about the Great Wall of China but why did they build such a long wall? It was to stop the Mongols from the north from invading China. Many nomadic tribes like the Mongols living in north China were a real headache as

they would sweep down to raid villages and towns, killing and robbing people. So the First Emperor Qin, the same one who wanted terracotta warriors, got the idea of building a long wall. He forced peasants to work at the wall and it was made of mud-brick and wood. Though it did not last very long, later kings liked the idea and over the next 1700 years, the wall was repaired and built again and again. Finally, the Ming Dynasty that ruled between the 14th and 17th centuries CE made it permanent by using stone and bricks. Today, tourists can walk around the wall as the Mongols have lost interest in invasions. The Great Wall is 8850 kilometres long and has a wide road on top and many watch towers for guards. It is now considered one of the Seven Wonders of the World, but the story that it can be seen from the moon is not true.

The American astronaut Alan Bean took a look from his spaceship and said it wasn't visible even a few miles into outer space!

Listen and Obey

The most influential thinker of ancient China was the philosopher Confucius, or Kong Fuzi, 'Master Kong' who shaped political thought for 2000 years. Confucius (551–479 BCE) was an adviser to the Zhou kings and a social reformer whose teachings became like a religion for the Chinese. He taught a new moral outlook based on kindness, respect and the importance of family. Subjects had to obey the ruler and the ruler was expected to care for his subjects. He created a code by which a society could live in a peaceful and orderly manner and he expected people to be truthful, obedient and disciplined. He sounds a bit like the headmaster of a school, doesn't he?

The most important thing for Confucius was that there should be peace and harmony in society, which meant that everyone should understand and accept their place in society and not try to be too ambitious or adventurous. This appealed to the kings and the rich who wanted common people to be obedient. Confucius also extended the idea of harmony to music and suggested that music should be taught in schools. However, only the sons of the rich could afford to go to school where they were taught the 'three perfections': painting, poetry and calligraphy.

The Chinese have always worshipped their ancestors as they believe that family members still watch over them after they die. So there are festivals during which the ancestors are worshipped, offered food and even gifts.

Another belief is that the world is divided into two elements: the yin and yang. Its symbol is a circle divided by a curving line into black and white. It is said that yin is weak, passive, dark and female; and yang is strong, active, male and bright—which really means that it was some man who came up with the idea in the first place. For example, the moon is yin and the sun is yang. These two elements balance the world and are used even in Chinese medicine for a balance of herbs and diet.

There was also the ancient faith of Taoism taught by the teacher Lao Zi that encouraged meditation, prayers and magic spells. Another interesting philosopher was Sun Zi who clearly liked fighting and wrote the *Art of War* that people read even today.

Buddhism is another belief prevalent in China. Buddhist monks travelling by the Silk Road arrived from India carrying the spiritual teachings of the Buddha and many people became Buddhists. From China, Buddhism travelled to Japan, Korea, Vietnam, Thailand and Cambodia. This led to two of the greatest travellers to visit India: the Chinese monks Fa Xian and Hsuan Tsang who came in search of rare Buddhist books at the universities of Nalanda and Takshashila. Their wonderful memoirs describe India during the reigns of Chandragupta Vikramaditya and Harsha Vardhana.

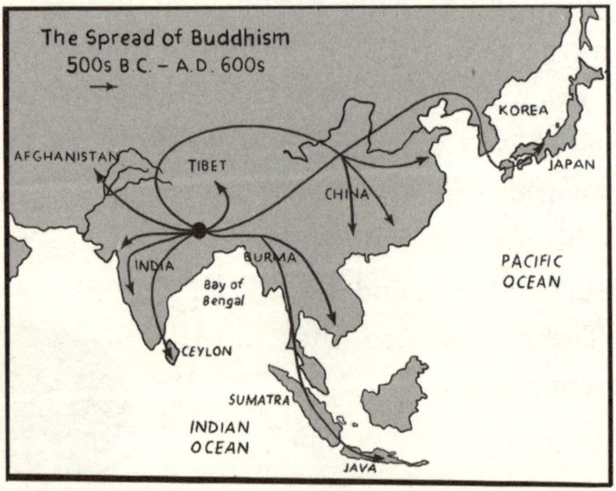

Board Exams? Oh No!

It was the Chinese who started the system of examinations to select the men who would work as government officials, and later Europe picked up the idea. Women, though, were not educated and so had no opportunities. The examination system began during the rule of the Zhou dynasty. The men had to give a very tough entrance examination and once selected, they would join the government and were known as the mandarin. Just like the bureaucrats of today, they loved to keep records and it was the Chinese mandarins who started the system of keeping copies of every record in triplicate!

The Silk Road

The oldest trade route in the world connected China with Europe. It also had a branch road moving south to India. In ancient times, only the Chinese knew how to make silk and as traders carried this precious textile along this road, it came to be called the Silk Road. At that time, silk was the most expensive textile in the world, bought by the rich in Egypt and Rome. The road covered over 4000 kilometres, connecting Han China with Rome. Caravans of traders with horses, camels and carts travelled up and down this road carrying many kinds of goods

The Silk Route

such as textiles, spices, ivory, incense, jewellery and porcelain.

Beginning in China, the Silk Road went through Central Asia, Persia, the Middle East and then on to Italy. The Chinese themselves did not travel all the way to Europe, instead they sold their goods at the border to Arab traders who also collected Indian goods like cotton textiles, jewellery and spices. This was how both goods and ideas travelled back and forth between Europe and Asia. The teachings of the Buddha spread to the Far East because of the traders

on the Silk Road. It was an extremely difficult journey over high mountain passes, deserts and forests and the caravans had to always be on guard against bandits. Both China and India became richer as they bought few European goods and instead took payment in gold. The Silk Road slowly went out of use when direct sea routes were discovered by the Portuguese explorer Vasco da Gama.

Zheng He

Zheng He was one of the greatest naval explorers of the world. He led a peaceful demonstration of Chinese naval power with 317 ships and 27,970 sailors and reached the coast of Africa. Along the way, he probably also visited the port of Cochin in Kerala. He did not try to conquer land, control the trade or capture slaves like the European countries would do later. His ships called junks were five times the size of the ones used by Vasco da Gama seventy years later.

A Trader, Are You?

Like all ancient civilizations, Chinese society was divided between various social classes according to their occupations: scholars, farmers, craftsmen and traders. The scholars gained the most respect because they could read and write, become mandarins and were advisers to the king. Next were the farmers who were valued as they grew crops to feed the people. Craftsmen came next, making pottery or metal ware, weaving silk and cotton for clothes. So the traders, who were often very rich, were considered the fourth or the lowest class. They did not like it at all and kept protesting to the kings.

Welcome to My Home

In China, people lived in large joint families where the oldest male member was the head of the house and everyone had to obey him. The Chinese worshipped their ancestors and every home had a shrine to them. Only the sons of rich families or scholars went to school, other boys just worked in the family profession—farming, crafts or trade. In schools they studied literature, science, mathematics, arts, music and the teachings of Confucius.

Girls were not educated and were expected to stay at home and do all the housework. One Han writer described the duties of women as, 'sewing, weaving and preparing food and wine for guests.' In poor families the women had to go out to work, usually as maids and cooks and those who had knowledge of medicinal herbs became doctors. Interestingly, most of the witchcraft and magic spells were done by sorceresses!

Come for Lunch!

Can you imagine a world without Hakka noodles or wanton soup? Fortunately, just like in India, every region in China has its own style of cooking and so we have a huge menu to choose from. The best-known cuisines are Anhui, Cantonese, Fujian, Hunan, Jiangsu, Shandong, Szechuan and Zhejiang.

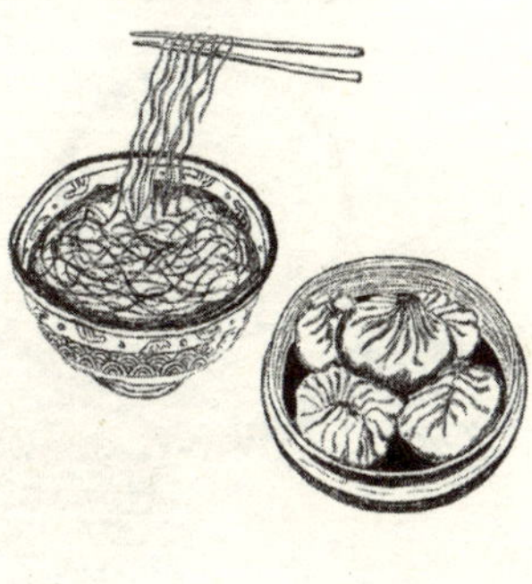

Historians believe the first noodles were cooked in China and slurped up using chopsticks. Archaeologists have found a bowl of noodles in Lajia in north-west China that could be 4000 years old! Some people believe that the Italian traveller Marco Polo, who visited China in the 15th century, described noodles and the Italians then created spaghetti. Of course, the Italian chefs do not agree! The Chinese call chopsticks kuai zi meaning 'small piece pickers' and have been using them since 1500 BCE when most of the world was still eating with their fingers. Chopsticks were originally made of wood, metal or bone, and nowadays they are also made of stainless steel and plastic.

Another delicious culinary creation is the dim sum which means 'touch the heart'. Dim sums are dumplings that are steamed or fried and have many kinds of fillings of meat and vegetables. By the 10th century CE, the Chinese were making 2000 kinds of dim sums. Can you imagine a dim sum festival where all of them were served? Yummm!

After noodles, the Chinese taught the world to drink tea. The story goes that in 2700 BCE, when Emperor Shen Nung's drinking water was being boiled, a few stray tea leaves fell into the pot.

He drank the water and found it very refreshing and tea was discovered. They call tea 'cha' and believe it is good for health. Modern doctors agree that it has beneficial antioxidants. There are six varieties of Chinese tea: red, black, green, wuloong, flower and brick. The brick tea is a mix of leaves pressed into a block. The Chinese never use sugar or milk in their tea; that recipe was invented by the British.

A Fashion Show

Legends say that silk was discovered by Empress Hsi Ling Shi of the Shang Dynasty when she realized that the worms eating the leaves of the mulberry trees in her garden wove a cocoon of very fine thread. This thread was then woven to

Women weaving silk

make a soft, light, lustrous textile called silk. The Chinese kept silk-making a secret for 3000 years and became hugely rich by selling it to the world.

Both men and women wore jackets, long robes, baggy trousers and tunics and they had rules about the colours of clothes. Only the emperor was allowed to wear yellow while poor people were ordered to wear blue and black. The long robe with loose sleeves that we see the Chinese wearing is called cheongsam for women and changsham for men. The poor of course could not afford silk or wool and wore cotton. Everyone kept their hair long and the women

had pretty hairdos decorated with jewelled pins and combs but the men just had a long plait.

The rich grew their nails very long to show that they did not do any manual labour and even wore pretty nail guards. Another truly weird fashion trend among women was the belief that the smaller the feet the prettier they are. So girls in rich families tied their feet in tight bandages to stop them from growing until the bones were curved and they could hardly walk. These bound feet were called 'lily feet' and the cruel custom continued into the 20th century.

No Spelling Mistakes!

The Egyptians made paper using a reed called papyrus while the Chinese used the pulp of bamboo fibres and no one really knows who came up with the idea first. In China, bamboo fibres were boiled, ground into a paste, dried in sheets on bamboo frames and then flattened by rollers. Before paper was invented, they used to write on rolls of silk and that made the books

The paper-making process

really expensive. With the introduction of paper books, they could sell the silk to other countries and make a profit!

In the beginning, books were all hand-written on silk or paper but then around 700 CE the Chinese invented block printing where wood tablets were carved with the letters and even illustrations. The tablet was dipped in ink and pressed on the paper to create the world's first printed books. And best of all, one tablet could print hundreds of books! Soon palaces and temples across the land had libraries and many more people could read books. The first book to be printed in the world was a Buddhist text called *Vajrachchedika Sutra* or the Diamond Sutra that was translated from Sanskrit into Chinese in 868 CE.

It is really tough to learn Chinese! The Chinese script which began 3200 years ago is extremely difficult to master because it is pictorial; that means instead of a group of alphabet, each word is a separate picture. So to write Chinese you have to learn the pictograph of a word as each word is a different character and you have to learn thousands of them. By 100 BCE, they had begun using reed pens and ink to write. The earliest samples of script were found carved on pieces of bone and tortoise shells called oracle bones as they were used to make predictions. A question would be carved on the bone and then the bone would be heated till it cracked and those cracks were studied for the answer.

The Chinese did not use clay or wax tablets like they did in Mesopotamia and Egypt. Paper was usually used only for important matters like government records, books on practical things like agriculture and textbooks. However, one kind of literature was allowed to be printed—poetry—though novels were frowned upon.

Here is a sample of 8th-century Chinese poetry:

'The moonlight shines on my bed;
It's like frost on the ground.
I lift my head to look at it;
Lie back again and think of my old home.'

—Li Po (701–762 CE)

They used pens, brushes and ink to write and soon artists transformed this into the art of calligraphy where simple words were written in such a beautiful way that they looked like paintings. They called calligraphy 'dancing on paper'. The ink was made from mixing the soot from lamps with glue and the calligrapher, too, used a set of brushes and pens. It took many years of training to become a calligrapher.

Fun and Games

There were many festivals like the Chinese New Year and the birthdays of their gods and goddesses. The Chinese celebrated with food, music and fireworks. They loved playing board games and the oldest one was first called Yi, and later Go. The Go board had a grid of seventeen squares and black and white counters were used.

The idea was to try and encircle and capture the other player's counters. Another popular Chinese game was Mah Jong played with rectangular tiles, which is played even today. And we are all familiar with the game called Chinese Checkers.

The First Inventors

Scientists and inventors were encouraged by the rulers and the Chinese led the world in inventions for centuries. Many of the things that we take for granted in our daily lives were invented by the Chinese. Take the wheelbarrow: by adding a handle to a two-wheeled cart, things could be carried easily for long distances and you did not need an animal to pull the cart. They even attached sails to wheelbarrows to make them go faster! Every time you use an umbrella or fly a kite, you should thank the Chinese. They also invented the sundial to tell the time and the seismometer to predict earthquakes

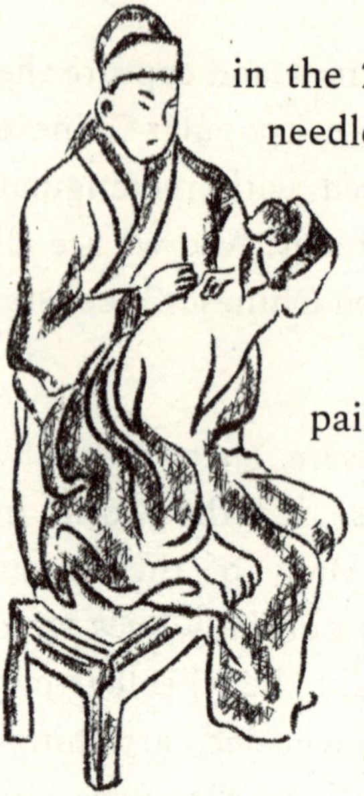

in the 2nd century. Doctors used needles placed in different parts of the body in acupuncture. Modern doctors think it works as an anaesthetic by releasing the brain's natural painkiller called endorphin.

The ancient healing practice of acupuncture

They discovered that rubbing an iron needle against a lodestone made it magnetic and it always pointed north and thus invented the magnetic compass. This helped in navigation when their ships travelled on the high seas. They also drew primitive maps using callipers to measure distances.

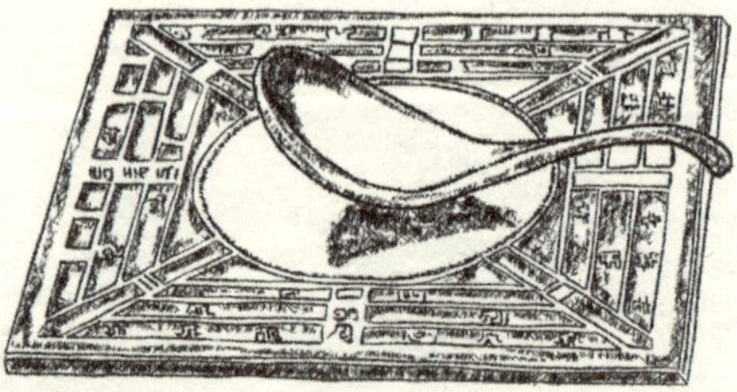

A compass

Can you imagine Diwali without fireworks? Fireworks were used by the Chinese first as military signals and then as weapons. They discovered that when they mixed potassium nitrate, sulphur and charcoal and put a match to it, it went whoosh!

Marco Polo (1254 CE–1324 CE)

Marco Polo and his father travelled from Venice, Italy, and reached the Chinese capital of Shangdu in 1275 CE. He was employed by the legendary Emperor Kublai Khan. He came back and wrote his memoirs that were read widely.

Crafted Art

Chinese craftsmen were famous across the world for their beautiful creations. Their most famous product was porcelain and it was so popular it was called china! Delicate bowls, plates and vases were moulded by potters, glazed and then painted in beautiful designs of flowers, landscapes and dragons.

Artists also painted silken scrolls and made lacquer jewellery, bowls and boxes. Carved

jade was another highly prized Chinese product. In India, Mughal kings had their food served in Chinese porcelain and jade bowls. They chose jade and green celadon because they believed that if the food was poisoned, the bowl would crack or change colour. Wonder if anyone ever tested the theory!

The rule of emperors continued till 1912, when the Chinese Revolution brought the Qing dynasty to an end. China is now a Communist state, ruled by the Communist Party of China.

THE CLEVER CHINESE

- As early as the 5th century BCE, Chinese warriors were flying flags made of silk to guide troops during a battle. They were often made in the shape of fierce dragons to scare the enemy.
- The Chinese were making cast-iron goods fifteen centuries before Europe.
- In the 13th century CE, the Italian traveller

Marco Polo reached the court of Emperor Kublai Khan in Shangdu. He brought back the first recipe for ice cream from China.

- The emperors encouraged martial arts like Kung Fu or Wushu and Tai Chi and the monks of the Shaolin temples were famous Kung Fu masters.
- Chinese coins had a hole in the middle so that they could be strung on a string to be carried. Guess what the coins were called—cash!
- The largest palace complex was built in Beijing in 15th century CE. The Forbidden City has 980 buildings and is a UNESCO World Heritage Site.
- Chinese astronomers said that solar eclipse happened when a dragon swallowed the sun while Indians said it was the asura called Rahu who swallowed it. The Chinese also worked out that the year was of 365.25 days.
- They had an agricultural calendar of twenty-four fortnights and these had interesting names. For example: Li Chun (Spring Begins), Jin Zhe (Excited Insects) and Bai Lu (White Dew).
- The archaeologist Aurel Stein found a temple on the Silk Road used by traders and it had painted images of the Buddha, images of the

Hindu gods Shiva and Brahma, many Iranian deities and local pagan gods. One temple for everyone!

- The most expensive porcelain was produced during the reign of the Ming Dynasty.

GREECE

TALKING OF IDEAS

(2000 BCE–350 BCE)

The first civilization to emerge in Europe was in Greece. The country stands on the Mediterranean Sea on the eastern edge of the continent and acts as a bridge between Europe and Asia. So it was influenced by both the Mesopotamian and Egyptian civilizations. Greece has many islands on the Ionian and Aegean seas and also mountainous regions on the mainland. The first farmers had settled in eastern Greece by 6000 BCE and they grew wheat and vegetables, kept sheep and went fishing in the sea. However, unlike civilizations such as Mesopotamia, Egypt and the Indus Valley, the Greek civilization was not based on a great river system but depended on the bounties of the sea. Activities like fishing, crafts and trade were the reason for their prosperity.

What makes the civilization that developed in Greece so unique is that it was not just about

progress in language, technology or science but also in ideas. The Greeks laid the foundation of Western civilization in areas of knowledge like in science, philosophy, art, literature and politics. From the beginnings of democracy and politics and political systems like elections and parliament to our ideas in science or theatre, we have to thank the Greeks, especially the leaders and philosophers of the state of Athens.

The Mighty Minoans

The first Greek civilization developed on the island of Crete around 3000 BCE and it lasted for nearly a thousand years. Crete had a legendary monarch called King Minos. When the remains of the civilization were discovered by the British archaeologist, Arthur Evans, he named it Minoan after him. Minos was probably a title for the king, like pharaoh. The myths of the creation of Crete said that the king of the gods Zeus fell in love with a beautiful princess named Europa. He turned himself into a bull and swam to Crete with her on his back and their son Minos became the king of Crete. Though if you think about it, it would have been easier for Zeus if he had turned himself into a whale or a dolphin! Because of this myth, the bull became a sacred animal and was worshipped by the Minoans. Later, the whole continent came to be called Europe after the princess.

The Minoans were great sailors and grew rich by trade and built several huge palaces on Crete. A town would then grow around each palace, with markets and the workshops of craftsmen. The largest palace was at Knossos. Its ruins have been discovered by archaeologists. Each palace

The dolphin frescoes

had its own king and royal family and they lived in rooms decorated with beautiful frescoes painted on the walls. Studying these paintings gives us an idea of the daily life of the people—the clothes and jewellery they wore; what they ate and even how they celebrated. Some of the frescoes also depict animals, fishes and birds and the cutest fresco shows a school of swimming dolphins jumping out of the blue sea with happy smiles on their faces.

The Minoans were a peaceful trading community that grew around palaces and not warlike fortresses with forbidding high walls. They grew prosperous through crafts like pottery, growing olives, making wine, fishing and trade. They traded with Egypt that was across the Mediterranean Sea and their frescoes and paintings on pottery show images of sailing ships. There are no images of warriors or people fighting or carrying weapons.

Half-human, Half-bull

As the Minoan script is yet to be deciphered, archaeologists have had to guess about their religion. Studying their sculpture and paintings, they think that the Minoans worshipped the bull. Many wall paintings show a religious ritual that was a dance where one man held a bull by the horns while another dancer ran, leaped and catapulted over a charging bull's back. Now that is quite a dangerous way to say your prayers!

There is also the legend of the Minotaur, a half-man, half-bull monster that lived deep in an underground maze called a labyrinth in the Knossos palace. The story goes that as the Minoans were the most powerful kingdom and dominated the region, they forced other Greek cities to send young men and women to become bull dancers and many were killed by the Minotaur. Then Theseus, the prince of Athens, went to Crete, killed the Minotaur and found his way back through the labyrinth with the help of a Cretan princess named Ariadne, who had fallen in love with the handsome Theseus.

Was It Atlantis?

Around 1600 BCE, the Minoan civilization declined possibly because of a devastating earthquake. A volcano on a nearby island called Thera exploded and parts of it sank into the sea and tidal waves and tsunamis may have swept over Crete. The famous Greek philosopher Plato wrote that there used to be an island called Atlantis that vanished under the sea, and for centuries since, the legend of Atlantis has fascinated explorers who have searched for it along the coast of Greece. Historians think Plato's Atlantis may be Thera. In 1960, excavations made at Thera unearthed a Minoan village under the ash and found houses, frescoes and pottery all perfectly preserved.

The Mycenaeans Are Coming!

Another reason for the decline of the Minoans was the rise of a warlike tribe called the Mycenaeans who invaded and conquered the Minoans. Like Crete, their civilization was also made of a group of cities and the biggest city was called Mycenae. Their palaces or walled fortresses were usually built on a high ground and were called the acropolis. The marketplace where people gathered was called the agora. The kings were buried in tombs with a lot of treasures just like in Egypt and archaeologists have found gold drinking cups, bowls, jewellery and fascinating death masks of kings. Unlike the peaceful Minoans, who were busy making money through trade, they were great warriors and many swords and spears have also been found in their graves. They may have won wars but you would agree that the peaceful Minoans had more fun in life.

Oh, Helen!

The famous Trojan War probably took place during this time, in 1250 BCE. Homer described this war in his epic poem *The Iliad*. It is the story of Helen, princess of Sparta, who was the most beautiful woman in the world. It was said that she was so beautiful that her face could launch a thousand ships! One wonders, how.

Helen was married to Menelaus, brother of Agamemnon the king of Mycenae. Then she fell in love with Paris, the prince of Troy, son of King Priam and eloped with him. The Greeks laid siege on the city of Troy and famous warriors on both sides like Achilles, Odysseus and Hector lined up to battle. The siege went on and on until after ten years of hanging around outside the walls of Troy, the Greeks came up with a plan.

The Greeks built a giant wooden horse and left it at the gate of Troy and sailed away in their ships as if they had given up and left for home. The Trojans thought the Greeks had retreated leaving the horse behind, and so they were fooled into carrying the horse inside the fortress. They

did not realize that there were soldiers hidden inside. These Greek soldiers came out at night, opened the gates and poured in and destroyed the city. Most of the Trojan warriors were killed and Helen was taken back to Greece.

Homer's next epic poem was *The Odyssey.* It described the adventures of a Greek warrior named Odysseus, who had fought in the Trojan War and thought up the plan with the Trojan horse. The war was over and he was now trying to get home, having many fantastic adventures on the way, including meeting Cyclops the one-eyed monster and the witch Medusa with snakes as hair. Homer is said to have been blind, and the poems were written a few centuries after the war around 700 BCE. The two epic poems and the

Cyclops

Medusa

Bible are the earliest books of European literature just as our Vedas and the epics Ramayana and Mahabharata are for India. The story of the Trojan War is interesting but scholars feel it must have been a battle for land. Only a poet could imagine people fighting for ten years for a princess.

Looking for Troy

In 1876, Heinrich Schliemann, an amateur archaeologist from Germany, found six royal tombs dated to 1600 BCE in modern Turkey and was convinced he had found the famous kingdom of Troy as well as the treasures of King Priam. Among the finds were pottery, a lot of jewellery, weapons and a chariot. There were five golden death-masks and he thought one of them was of King Agamemnon but he was mistaken. The mask was made in 1550 BCE and the war took place three centuries later. There is a photograph of Schliemann's wife wearing all the jewellery they had discovered. The treasures vanished during World War II but have recently surfaced in Russia.

Let's Meet at the Agora

As the Mycenaean civilization began to decline there was a time of chaos and confusion in Greece called the Dark Ages when they even forgot how to write! Luckily it was followed by the finest period of its history, with the rise of famous cities like Athens, Sparta, Argos and Corinth. These city states were called Polis—from where we get the word politics—as the political system was first developed here. Each city state was ruled by a small group of rich noblemen called aristocrats and this system is called an oligarchy. Sometimes one powerful man ruled alone and he was called the tyrant.

Each city had a hill-top citadel protected by high walls called the acropolis or 'high city'. It contained temples and homes of the powerful aristocratic families. A central open space called agora was surrounded by the homes of ordinary

The agora

citizens. The agora was the main marketplace where there were shops and farmers and fishermen sold their produce and the day's catch. Slavery was accepted by Greek society as it was in most ancient civilizations, and slaves were also sold here. There were moneylenders called 'table men' as they sat at tables ready to give

The acropolis

loans or exchange money. These men were the first bankers of Europe. The agora was the main gathering place for people, and festivals and processions went up to the acropolis from here.

Each city state developed in its own way. Athens was a peaceful society that was culturally rich with philosophers, art and theatre and it had a democratic system where officials were elected by the people and not appointed by the ruler. In contrast, the city state of Sparta had a very war-like character. Here, arts and philosophy were discouraged and good health and physical strength were prioritized, and even young girls were given athletic training. All the men had to join the army and young boys were put in training schools where they faced very tough conditions. The boys were in constant physical training, leading a very simple life, eating bad food and being disciplined all the time. The word 'spartan' comes from this system and Sparta.

Time to Vote

As the tyrants were ruling the city states, the traders began to protest. They were rich and paid much of the taxes but they were not allowed any power. So a new system of government and laws were gradually developed in Athens that became an early form of democracy, a system in which a government is run by a group of officials with the approval of the people and not a king. In fact, the word democracy comes from two Greek words: demos, people and kratos, rule. Once democracy was established, people would gather in the agora and vote for or against any action by the government. This was an early stage of democracy where power lies with the people through their right to vote.

Of course, it was very different from our idea of democracy. For instance, the right to vote was limited. Only some men were given the title of citizens and they could vote; no women, slaves or anyone who was not born in Athens was given the title. The citizens met in the open space of the agora where the leaders of the city put up their proposals and they all had the right to say yes or no. Citizens took part in politics, joined the army, became officials and did jury duty. In Athens we also see the first jury of a group of citizens passing judgment on legal cases instead of a king.

The citizens of Athens were first given the right to vote by an aristocrat named Cleisthenes in 508 BCE. The assembly of citizens met every ten days on a hill called Pnyx. There were debates and the vote was taken when at least 600 citizens were gathered there. At a time when everywhere in the world there were kings, Athens had given the right to rule to its people. In Athens, and later in other Greek cities, power lay in an assembly of people like today's parliament. This political system of democracy is Greece's greatest gift to the world.

Classical Athens

The greatest of the city states was Athens, which is the capital of modern Greece. Between 500 and 350 BCE, some of the greatest thinkers, artists and scholars lived here, like the philosophers Socrates, Plato and Aristotle and the mathematicians, Euclid and Archimedes. Beautiful buildings like the Parthenon were built and sculptors created marble images of not just gods and goddesses but also of ordinary people.

The cities had palaces, temples, schools and busy markets. Exciting masked-plays were enacted in the amphitheatres and many athletic competitions were held, the most famous being the Olympic Games. The Parthenon was a temple to the goddess Athena who was the goddess of war and the patron goddess of the city. The two most powerful cities were Athens and Sparta and there was intense rivalry between them. They fought the Peloponnesian wars between 431 and 404 BCE that ruined both the cities and brought the great period of city states to an end.

Only Men Allowed!

Society in the city states was divided into citizens and non-citizens. The citizens were the people who had a say in the government and they were only those men who had been born in the city. The women and slaves had no rights and neither did the people born outside the city who were called Metics. Sometimes these Metics were rich traders or craftsmen but still they had no rights as citizens. It was very different from what we think of as citizenship in a democracy, where everyone is equal in society.

The rich men led pretty easy lives, attending parties, watching plays and sports. They were surprisingly comfortable with their bodies and were often depicted in the nude in sculptures. The athletes at the games competed naked and then their portraits were carved very realistically in marble like the famous sculpture of a discus thrower. Unlike the Egyptian sculptures that were very formal and idealized, with all the pharaohs looking the

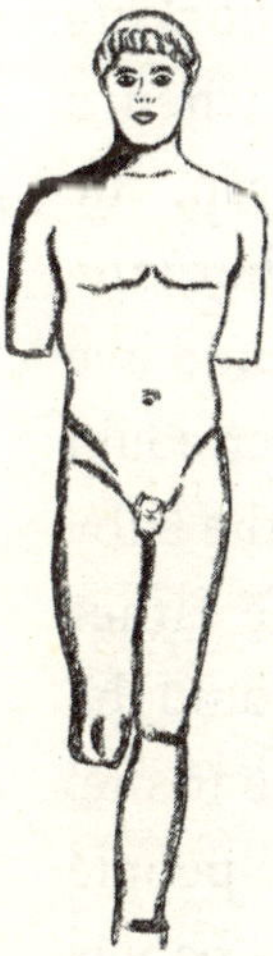

same, the Greek artists depicted the human body and facial expressions in a realistic manner with muscles and natural poses. Of course, the women were shown all draped in clothes from head to toe.

Women Stay at Home

It was not easy being a woman in Greece as they had no freedom at all. At this time, women in Egypt lived much freer lives and they even had women pharaohs. A Greek woman had to be obedient to the men in her life—first her father and brothers, then her husband and finally even her sons. They were not allowed to go to school and were mainly taught to cook, spin, weave cloth, run the house and raise the children. One shocking practice was that when a baby girl was born, the father decided her fate, whether she would live or die; the mother could say nothing. So if the baby was weak or if the father was poor, she would be left on the hillside to die. At times other people would take these babies

home and the girls would become slaves when they grew up.

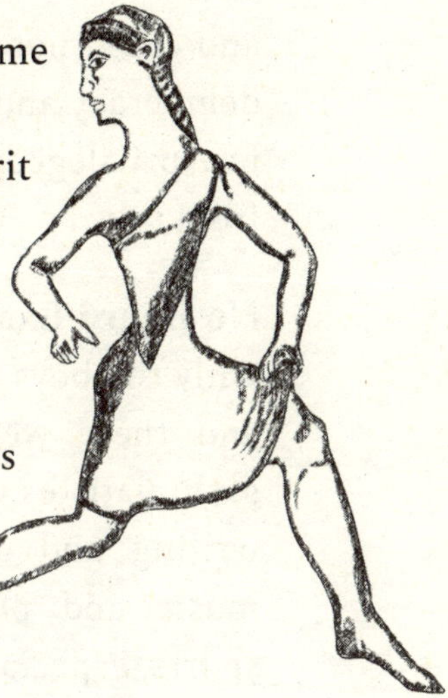

Greek women could not inherit any money or property or take part in the political meetings in the agora. The only exception were the women of Sparta who were encouraged to learn sports so that they could bear healthy sons who would become good soldiers. So they ran in races, did physical exercise wearing short skirts and the people of the other cities did not approve at all. There is a famous sculpture of a young Spartan girl in a short skirt running, exactly the way sportswomen run today.

Living a Slave

Slaves were common and no one questioned the practice. Most slaves worked in homes while female slaves were also dancers and entertainers called hetaira. Some slaves were educated and became teachers called pedagogues. Close to a quarter of the population of Athens were slaves and of course they had no rights, were not paid for their services, could not own property, marry without the permission of their owners and could not vote—here was a state talking of democracy and equal rights but only for a select few privileged men. Luckily, we have come far from that.

No Board Exams!

Only the boys from rich families went to school and there were three types of schooling. A grammatistes was a teacher who taught reading, writing and arithmetic. A kitharistes taught music and poetry and a paidotribes taught sports, especially athletics. Rich people at times hired an educated slave called paidagogos who would supervise a boy's education. The English word pedagogy, meaning the science of teaching, comes from that. So it must have been the grammatistes who gave the kids class tests and homework to do.

We think of a gymnasium as a place where athletes practice but in ancient Greece they were centres of both sports and learning. These were colleges where professors of higher learning called sophists—like Socrates, Plato and Aristotle—met young students for lectures and debates and students were encouraged to ask questions. Many important political and philosophical ideas were discussed and developed at these gymnasia.

Thinking Smart

Greece was the first civilization to focus on ideas. During the time of the city states there were great advances not just in politics but also astronomy, geography, history and mathematics. The Greek scholars and teachers were called philosophers, meaning 'lovers of knowledge' and that meant they asked questions and tried to find answers. Philosophy was the study of ideas and asking questions like 'What is the meaning of life? What is right and wrong? What is the true meaning of happiness?' The questions look simple but try to answer them and you may find yourself getting very confused!

Socrates (469–399 BCE) was an Athenian philosopher who was interested in studying goodness and what makes people happy. He did not give lectures, instead had debates and discussions with his followers and because he asked uncomfortable questions, he was unpopular with the politicians. Socrates was also an atheist

who refused to believe in gods and was accused of impiety. The rulers of Athens tried him in court and sentenced him to death; he was ordered to drink a poison called hemlock.

One of the greatest teachers at Athens was Plato (429–347 BCE), a pupil of Socrates. Socrates had insisted that every idea had to be debated in his gymnasium but did not write down any of them. This was done by Plato and this system of debates is the basis of democracy where we discuss issues in parliament. Plato began an academy that was the first university in the world. He wrote *The Republic*, a book that describes an ideal government where citizens have equal rights.

Plato's pupil was Aristotle (384–322 BCE) who disagreed with Plato's theories on politics and was more interested in observing the world and developed subjects like botany and biology and wrote about plants and animals after studying them carefully. Aristotle also taught Alexander of Macedonia who conquered Egypt, the Middle East and Persia and then came and fought King Porus in India. During his travels, Alexander used to send cuttings of plants and flowers to Aristotle.

Eureka and Ouch!

Ancient Greece produced amazing scholars in many fields whose work survives till today. Herodotus was the first scholar to write a correct record of events that we call history. He visited places and interviewed people who had witnessed important events such as battles and wrote about them. He is called the 'father of history'.

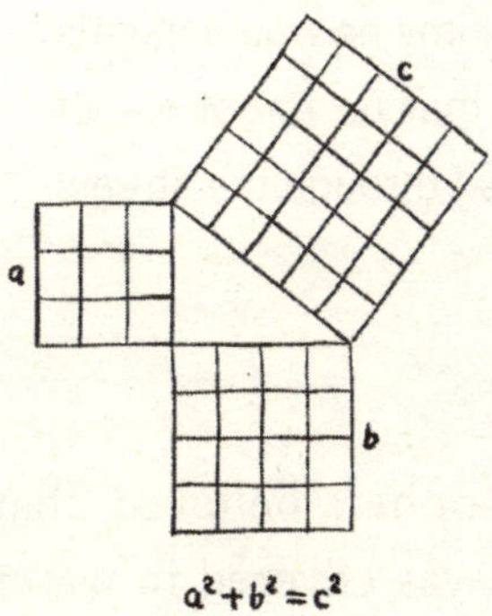

The Pythagoras Theorem

The most famous mathematicians were Euclid, Archimedes and Pythagoras who set out the basic rules of mathematics. The astronomer Aristarchus said that the earth revolved around the sun when everyone believed it was the other way round. Anaxagoras said that the moon had no light of its own and reflected the sun's light and that solar eclipses happened because the moon was blocking the sun. Of course, no one believed these astronomers and their theories were soon forgotten.

Archimedes

The Greek mathematicians looked for answers to everything through numbers like the geeks of today. King Heiron of Syracuse wanted to find out if his jeweller had put the correct amount of gold in a crown. To calculate the density of the metal Archimedes needed to know the volume of the crown. While lying in a full bathtub he realized his body displaced water and by putting the crown in water and measuring the volume he would get the answer. He got so excited that he forgot to put on any clothes and ran naked through the streets yelling 'Eureka!' or 'I got it!'.

Anaximander, a philosopher, believed that in the beginning the earth was covered in water and humans developed from fish. Hippocrates was a famous doctor who changed the way sick people were treated: earlier people would pray to the gods when they became sick, but he decided to examine the patient, diagnose the illness through symptoms and then give herbal medicines. In India we had physicians like Charaka and Shushruta who were doing the same. So these men were the first doctors to poke into an aching stomach!

Hippocrates

Poetry, Plays But No Pop Music

The English alphabet that we use today has developed from the Greek alphabet that had twenty-four letters. Some of them look and sound pretty similar like alpha for A or beta for B, but some were quite strange like xi which was pronounced as 'ks' or psi pronounced as 'ps'. Try pronouncing them, it is not easy!

The most popular writers in Greece were poets and playwrights and the two most famous epic poems are *The Iliad* and *The Odyssey* by Homer. The Greeks wrote the first dramas, tragedies and comedies often with an orchestra

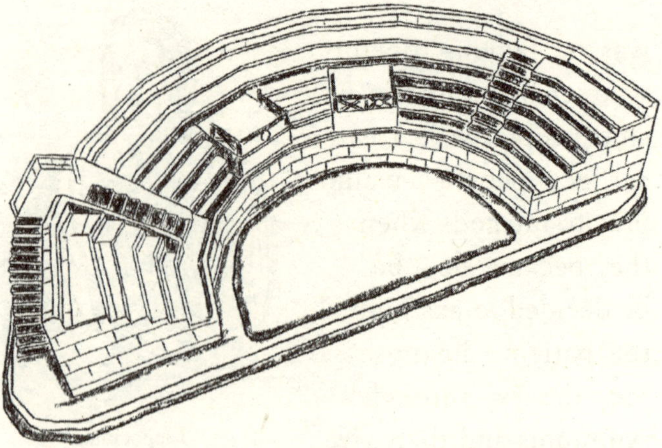

An amphitheatre where plays were performed

The masks used by actors during plays

singing in the background. Among the most popular playwrights were Aeschylus, Sophocles and Euripides and their works have survived and are performed even today. Aristophanes was a leading writer of funny plays called Attic comedy that was very popular.

The plays, both tragedies and comedies, were performed in large open-air theatres, called amphitheatres, with a semicircle of seats, a stage in front and a space where the chorus stood and sang. Only men acted in the plays, so they also played the female roles. As the actors' faces were not easy to see from the back seats, they wore large masks that showed the character they were playing. Sometimes they had two-faced masks, one face showing a happy expression and the other a sad one, and with a quick flick of the wrist they would change them. As there were no microphones, they would say their lines loudly and act with their bodies. In front, the chorus would sing with musicians playing instruments like drums, the lyre and the kithara that looks a bit like a square guitar.

The Great Games

The Greeks had no football or cricket World Cups but they had famous games like the one at Olympia and even today the world's biggest athletic event

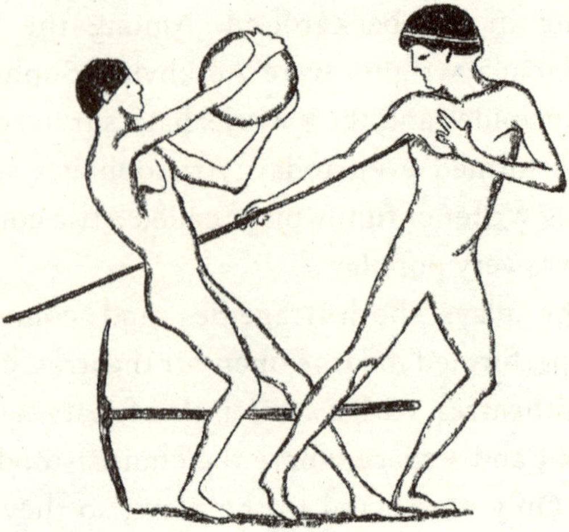

is called the Olympics. There were four big sports festivals in Greece—at Olympia, Delphi, Argos and Corinth, all held to honour the god Zeus. The one at Olympia was the oldest and the most famous. People travelled from as far away as Egypt and Spain to watch the games and the winners became instant stars with their sculptures being made. Athletes trained for years to compete in events like races, wrestling, throwing the spear and discus, and chariot races. The hardest challenge was the pentathlon in which the athletes had to compete in running, long jump, discus-throw, javelin-throw and wrestling.

The winners did not get a medal like they do today, just a wreath made of laurel leaves that was placed on their head. Heralds were sent to other cities with invitations but in the arena no woman was to be seen anywhere. The first Olympic took place in 776 BCE but over time it died out. It was revived in 1876 CE by a Frenchman Baron Pierre de Coubertin as the modern games. Even today the Olympic flame is lit in Olympia in a lovely ceremony by young women in traditional Greek costume and then the torch is carried across continents to the location of that year's games.

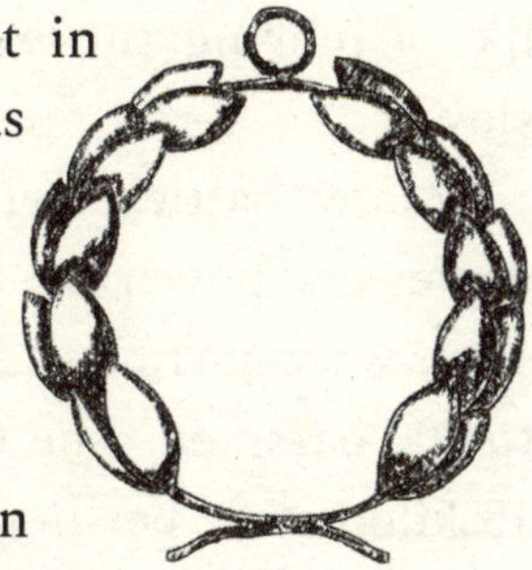

Okay, Let's Fight!

The city states were constantly at war with each other and so each had their own armies. The soldiers of the elite infantry were called hoplites. They wore full armour with helmets and metal covering for their arms, chest and legs. They carried shields, long spears and short swords. The hoplites moved in a formation called a phalanx. It was a tight group of men in rows of eight with their shields held before them and the spears pointing in front or above them looking a bit

like a moving turtle—and they moved just as slowly!

Many battles were fought on sea and the navies had powerful ships called triremes. These ships were narrow and fast, with a long row of up to 200 oarsmen. The triremes could move up to 15 kilometres per hour and were light and easy to manoeuvre as during a battle the archers and swordsmen stood on the deck, ready for a fight. The front of the ship was pointed and covered in metal to ram the enemy ship and make a hole on its side.

Going to the Temple

The Greeks worshipped many gods and goddesses like Zeus, Aphrodite and Apollo. They built huge temples where they placed the images of the deities made of marble, metal, wood or ivory. There were many festivals with processions made up of musicians and dancers coming from the temple to the agora. One of the biggest festivals that took place every four years in Athens was Panathenaea to honour Athene, the goddess of the city. During the celebrations, a procession of worshippers would take a new dress for Athene to the temple. This temple still stands on a hill in modern Athens and is called the Parthenon. Sadly, the image of Athene no longer stands there.

The architects built beautiful, pillared stone temples and the sculptors chiselled magnificent images. Many of these sculptures have survived till today and we look at them in amazement because they are carved so beautifully. Just like in Egypt, these temples had priestesses called oracles who claimed to be able to hear the gods. So when people asked any questions, they would answer for the god and if the prediction came true, people would offer gifts to the temple. The most famous oracle was at the temple of Apollo at Delphi and the oracle was called Pythia. The Greek conqueror Alexander went to Delphi before he started on his campaign to conquer the world. No one really knows what Pythia told him because Alexander never revealed it to anyone.

The Temple at Delphi

GORGEOUS GREECE!

- The Greeks called themselves Hellenes. The Romans, who were greatly influenced by them, called them the Greeks.
- All European scripts developed from ancient Greek alphabets that had both vowels and consonants.
- There are many words we use in English that come from the Greeks: politics, democracy,

academy, gymnasium, symposium, ostracise. Though in Greece, a symposium was a formal drinking party, not a solemn meeting.

- Schools taught a subject called rhetoric: how to write and deliver speeches.
- Greece produced beautiful pottery in red with paintings in black that showed the life of the people: women dancing and men drinking wine. The English poet John Keats wrote the poem 'Ode to a Grecian Urn' about them.
- Like in Egypt, the kings were buried with a golden death mask.
- The English writer Mary Renault wrote the books *The Bull from the Sea* and *The King Must Die* about the legend of Theseus and the Minotaur of Crete.
- Athens was named after Athene, the goddess of war and wisdom. She gave the city a sacred olive tree. Today Greece grows many kinds of olives and uses olive oil for cooking.
- Socrates, who was accused of corrupting young minds, was married to Xanthippe and spent his life complaining of her bad temper.
- Aristotle's school was called lyceum and he focussed on science, mathematics and the arts and less on philosophy.
- The teacher Epicurus shocked society by teaching women and slaves.

- The British ambassador to the Ottoman Empire Lord Elgin took away the sculptures from the Acropolis in Athens and they are now displayed in the British Museum in London. The Greeks want the Elgin marbles back.

Rome
A World Empire
(753 BCE–1453 CE)

Around 3000 years ago, a tribe called the Latins arrived at the banks of the Tiber River in Italy. Here they began to grow crops and soon a group of villages flourished on the side of the seven hills. This is the beginning of the great city of Rome that became the capital of the Roman Empire and the first civilization to conquer all of Europe.

The Roman Empire became one of the greatest empires of the ancient world, stretching from England in the West to Syria in the Middle East and including all of Italy, Spain, France and also Egypt, Libya and Morocco in North Africa. At its heyday, all the land around the Mediterranean Sea was part of the empire. Rome became very rich and was the greatest city in Europe, filled with beautiful buildings, busy markets and majestic sculptures. At the zenith of its power, the Roman Empire had 60

million subjects and Roman culture influenced the culture of many countries. The empire was the main market for goods from China and India that were transported by merchants along the Silk Road.

The Divine Twins

There is a fascinating myth about how Rome was built and it came from the imagination of a historian named Titus Livius, known as Livy, who cleverly mixed up the story of the Greek epic poem *Iliad* and the histories of the kingdom of Troy and the city of Rome.

Livy wrote that a mythical Greek hero who fought in the Trojan War named Aeneas came to Italy and married a Latin princess. Their

descendants were twin boys called Romulus and Remus. The boys' wicked uncle Amulius who wanted to be king, decided to kill them and ordered that they should be drowned in the Tiber but his men took pity on the babies and set them afloat in a cradle. When they drifted ashore, the twins lived in a cave on the Palatine Hills and a she-wolf fed them her milk till a shepherd and his wife found them and brought them up.

Once they grew up, the boys killed their evil uncle and then started building a new city. While working, they had a violent argument about who would become the first king and Romulus killed Remus. Thus, Romulus became the first king of the new city which was named Rome after him. According to Livy—who was clearly more of a storyteller than a historian—all this happened in 753 BCE. It is possible that the first king of Rome belonged to the tribe called Etruscans who worshipped the wolf.

Floating on a River

The myth of a baby being placed in a basket and floated down a river seems to be common to many civilizations. Like Romulus and Remus, there was the baby Moses, later a leader of the

Jews, who was abandoned on the River Nile by an Egyptian princess. Then in India there was the hero of the Mahabharata, Karna who was placed in the waters of the Yamuna by his mother Kunti. Now who came up with this plot first?

The Mysterious Etruscans

The Romans adopted many ideas from other civilizations. Their idea of democracy and a republic was very similar to the Greek republics as the Romans were great admirers of the Greek civilization. They were also influenced by an earlier culture of north Italy of a people called the Etruscans and the Sabines of the south. The Etruscans had city states that flourished between 800 and 400 BCE but we know little about them. Many of the things that we think of as Roman like painting frescoes on the walls of homes; the aqueducts; chariot races and gladiator fights; and even the Roman male dress called the toga originally came from the Etruscans.

We Are Republicans

In the beginning the city had kings but by 510 BCE, Rome had become a republic, which meant that it was ruled by its citizens led by two men called consuls. In Rome, society was divided into two groups of people: citizens and non-citizens. The citizens had the power and privileges and in return they had to vote in the elections, fight in the army and at times work as officials in the government. Like in Athens, to be a citizen you had to be born in the city of citizen parents and of course citizenship was reserved for men; women, children and slaves could not be citizens, neither could people born outside the city.

The rich citizens called themselves the patricians and they belonged to powerful families, and the rest were called plebeians. Three hundred patrician men were elected to the senate, which was a bit like our parliament, where the senators met and decided on how the government should be run and usually the plebeians had little say in the matter. The two consuls who headed the senate were always patrician men. The patricians had a lot of expenses as they had to pay their supporters and build public buildings and at times they went bankrupt. So to be a successful politician you had to belong to the right family, be a male and also very rich!

The plebeians were poorer people like shopkeepers, soldiers, labourers and craftsmen. They had no power and soon the richer businessmen who were paying a lot of taxes began to protest. When the plebeians threatened to leave Rome and build their own cities, the senate got worried and decided that the plebeians could elect two officers to the senate called tribunes. Gradually more plebeians were allowed into the senate and the first plebeian consul was elected in 366 BCE. The Roman Republic ruled by a senate lasted from 509 BCE to 27 BCE. After that monarchy took over and Rome was ruled by emperors.

Hail Caesar!

In the 2nd century BCE, things became rather chaotic in Rome. The Roman army had been sent out to conquer Europe and that meant that many poor farmers had been forced by the senate to join the army. Many rich men exploited this situation and bought their lands at cheap prices. This made the farmers furious and they began to protest, leading to much unrest between the patricians and plebeians in Rome. A general named Gnaeus Pompeius Magnus and his friend Julius Caesar took advantage of this unrest and grabbed power. Gnaeus

Julius Ceasar

was popularly called Pompey the Great because clearly his name was difficult to pronounce!

A skilled orator and popular general, Julius Caesar came from the old Julian family that claimed they descended from the goddess Venus. He had conquered Gaul (modern France) and invaded Britain and now he made an attempt at becoming the dictator of Rome. He became popular by passing laws to help the poor and then he defeated Pompey and defied the senate. He made himself the emperor for life which meant that the senate had no power. It was Julius Caesar who conquered Egypt and had children with Queen Cleopatra. After ruling for three years, in 44 BCE, he was assassinated by a group of senators led by his friend Brutus who were afraid he was becoming too powerful.

'Et Tu Brutus?'

Shakespeare wrote an unforgettable play about the assassination of Julius Caesar on the Ides of March or the 15th of March, 44 BCE. In the play, while dying, Julius Caesar looks at his friend Brutus and asks in surprise, 'You too Brutus?' The dialogue is still used as a comment on betrayal.

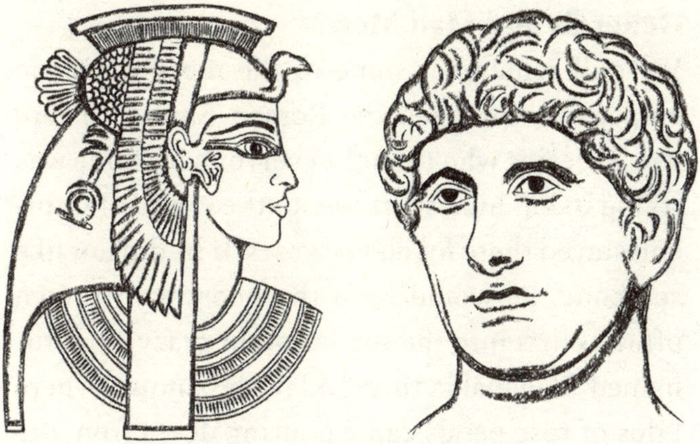

Cleopatra and Mark Anthony

Killing Julius Caesar did not really help, as a civil war followed and the senate failed to stop the rise of powerful generals Mark Anthony and Octavian, who then began to fight with each other. Mark Anthony and Cleopatra, who later teamed up, were defeated at the Battle of Actium and both committed suicide. After that, Rome was ruled by emperors and the republic came to an end. The second emperor was Julius Caesar's nephew Octavian who now named himself Augustus. A long and complicated list of emperors followed as many of these emperors liked being addressed as Caesar. Under the emperors, the Roman Empire lasted for five centuries from 27 BCE to 450 CE.

Generals and Mad Men

We still remember some of the more eccentric emperors who ruled the Roman Empire. There was Tiberius who thought everyone in Rome was trying to kill him, so he fled to the island of Capri and stayed there for eleven years. If he did not like someone, he would have the poor man thrown off the cliffs into the sea. Another crazy emperor named Elagabalus threw a lavish banquet where kilos of rose petals came pouring down from the ceiling over the guests. The problem was that there were so many petals that some guests were smothered to death under them!

The emperor Caligula was quite mad too. He declared that he was god and once tried to get his horse elected to the senate. Then he declared war on the sea god Neptune and ordered his soldiers to attack the Mediterranean Sea—that must have really confused the fish!

The worst of them all was the bloodthirsty Nero who murdered his mother and wife. It was said that when there was a great fire in Rome, he was busy playing a lyre and singing, instead of helping the people. He believed he was a great singer and would invite people to his concerts where he would sing on and on. No one was allowed to leave before the end and so in sheer desperation people would pretend to die so that they could be carried out.

Of course, there were some good emperors too, like Tiberius' nephew Claudius, Justinian and Nerva who ran an efficient empire.

The Ghost City

In 79 CE, the volcano Vesuvius erupted and covered the city of Pompeii in lava and volcanic ash. Most people had managed to escape the eruption but about 2000 people died. Pompeii stood near the modern city of Naples and it

Pompeii city

stayed buried under this ash for over 1500 years till an excavation in 1748. What was revealed was a ghost town with everything lying intact: homes, markets, streets, furniture and even the pots and pans in the kitchens. Pompeii is of great help to archaeologists because it has preserved the life of that time perfectly.

Not Built in a Day

By the time of the reign of Emperor Trajan (53–117 CE), Rome had over a million people living in the city. The emperors built splendid buildings made of marbles, and filled the city with statues. There were palaces, mansions, the curia where the senate met, temples, open squares called piazzas and markets. Augustus said proudly that he found a city of bricks and left it in marble and other emperors all competed to build more and more fancy buildings. The centre of Rome was called the forum and it had the curia and the law courts called basilica; they were built so well that 2000 years later many of them still stand and tourists look open-mouthed at them.

However, living in Rome was far from easy. The ordinary people lived in tall rickety wooden buildings of many floors on narrow, dirty streets and as there was no regular police force there was little law and order. There were no streetlights and the city would plunge into darkness at sunset. So people would usually stay at home after it got dark as the streets were full of pickpockets and robbers. The wealthy would move around with guards. The poet Juvenal said that as there was no guarantee you would come back alive, it would be foolish to go out after dark without making a will.

There were many poor people for whom the government gave a dole of free grain and over two hundred thousand people lived on the free food. There was no running water and people had to collect water from fountains. There was no proper system of garbage collection and in poor areas the lanes were often piled high with stinking garbage. They clearly did not know about the Indus Valley cities. Often, as people walked down a street someone would drop garbage on their heads from a window above, so Romans usually walked looking up!

The tiny taverns where the poor came to eat were called popinae and men would gather there to gossip, play dice and drink wine. Rome was a very noisy city with vendors calling, the traffic of horses and creaking carts and street entertainers. There would be the sound of hammers coming from the workshops, smoke billowing out from

A bath in Rome

the bakeries and beggars calling out to passers-by. Most homes did not have bathrooms so people would go to public baths that had pools with hot and cold water. Women would usually go to the bath houses in the mornings and the men in the afternoons. The baths were luxurious with the caldarium which was the hot pool; the tepidarium with cool water; and frigidarium with cold water. The expensive ones had snack bars, gardens, lounges and even libraries.

In winter, people would light fires in their rooms to keep warm and often the houses would catch fire. Emperor Augustus organized fire fighters called vigiles who were the first fire brigade in the world but all they had were buckets and hand pumps so they were not too good at putting out the fires. In 64 CE, there was a devastating fire and most of Rome was burnt to the ground and people blamed Emperor Nero. They believed he wanted to grab their land to build more palaces.

Great Builders

Roman architects and engineers were an extremely talented lot and constructed buildings, bridges and aqueducts which are still standing 2000 years later. This is because they invented a type of concrete called pozzolana that was made by mixing volcanic ash, crushed stones and water.

A typical viaduct

It was used to fill the walls and made them so strong that a building could have many storeys. They worked out the way to build a dome and an arch and used fired bricks.

The Romans built roads raised above the ground called viaducts that were a bit like our flyovers. Aqueducts were structures that could bring water across hills with the water flowing along raised stone channels. The aqueducts were an engineering marvel and during its heyday, 220 million gallons of fresh water was piped into the city for baths and fountains. Then Rome got an underground drainage system, just like the Indus Valley cities and the largest sewer was called Cloaca Maxima. It was so huge that one city engineer had to inspect it by sailing in a boat through its dark passages. It must have been quite a smelly trip!

Join the Army and See the World

The Roman Empire was the largest empire in the world stretching from Britain in the west to Syria in the east; from Germany in the north to Egypt in the south. From east to west, it stretched for 4000 kilometres. By 117 CE, the Roman Empire had a population of 50 million people. All the modern countries that surround the Mediterranean Sea, including those of North Africa, were conquered

Roman soldiers

by the Romans. They could manage it because of their army which was an efficient war machine. Men joined the army for twenty to twenty-five years and were trained well. The soldiers were called legionaries and they would march up to 30 kilometres a day, carrying all their heavy weapons. The soldiers were paid well and after retirement, they were given land and money, so it was considered a good career.

The Romans were great road builders and the army built the roads and bridges across the empire so that they could travel easily. By 200 CE, they had built 85,000 kilometres of roads

An old Roman road

across the empire—all constructed by men, and not machines. The roads not only helped the army to move but also in developing trade. Soon merchant's caravans were travelling all across the empire on these roads. Many modern roads in Europe still follow the route of the ones built by the Romans. The roads were very sturdy with layers of crushed stones mixed with concrete topped by larger stones but they were not smooth like modern roads so riding a chariot over them must have been a pretty teeth-rattling experience.

In every new area the Romans conquered, they would set up a fortress where a garrison would be stationed and so Roman soldiers travelled the world. These fortresses became the foundation of cities with baths, temples, law courts, markets, food shops and hospitals. The city of London was first a Roman city called Londinium which was the capital of the province of Brittanica.

Mum, Dad and Us

Romans had large joint families, similar to those in India, with grandparents, parents, uncles, aunts and cousins all living under one roof. The family was headed by the senior-most male called the paterfamilias and every one had to obey him. Rich families owned a number of slaves who did most of the work, so the women ran

the household and managed the family business when the men went off to wars. The parents arranged the marriages of the children, choosing the bride or groom from families they approved of and at times, girls as young as twelve years old were married. The bride would wear a wedding ring and her family would have to give a dowry. This sounds familiar, doesn't it?

Schooldays

Both boys and girls went to schools called ludus, where they were taught from dawn to noon. Usually, a school was a room with one teacher and about a dozen pupils learning the basics such as reading, writing and arithmetic. They wrote on tablets of wax using a pointed pen called stylus and would wipe the wax to use it again. Children left school when they were eleven years old, and girls did not study any more, but at least in the well-off families the girls could read and write. We have some lovely paintings and sculptures showing women and girls reading books and writing on tablets.

A Roman woman reading a book

The schools were modelled on the Greek ones and many Greek teachers came to Rome to teach. Some boys went to secondary school called Grammaticus where they studied Greek and Latin literature, history, geography, astronomy, mathematics, music and athletics. Then most of the young men trained to join the army and later joined politics while the girls prepared to get married. Men did not really approve of women being educated and the poet Juvenal said, 'I hate a woman who reads.' Clearly, some well-read woman had defeated him in an argument!

A Slave's Life

Slavery was rather common in Rome. Rich families had mansions in the city and huge estates in the countryside. They owned many slaves who did all the work in the house and at their farms. Many slaves were brought from the provinces, others were born in slave families and some were prisoners of war. The slaves who were educated became teachers, doctors and librarians but most of them led very hard lives. In the cities, the slaves worked

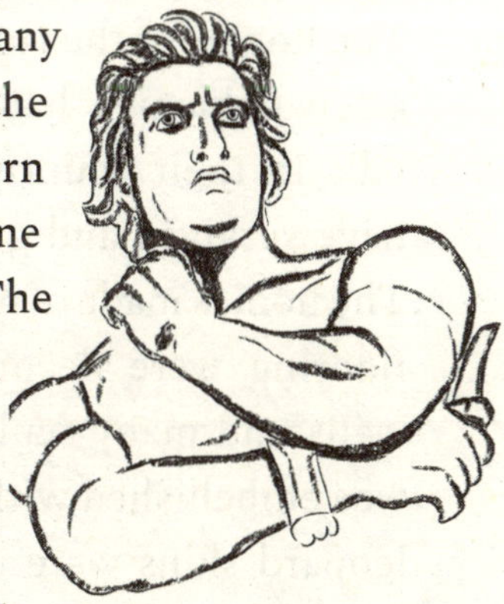
Spartacus, the Roman gladiator

in homes but they were also forced to work under terrible conditions in farms and mines. There was a famous rebellion by slaves led by Spartacus who had been forced to fight as a gladiator. In 73 BCE, his army of 90,000 slaves won some battles but were ultimately defeated.

A few slaves were freed while others saved money and bought their freedom, so some were probably able to earn some money but they did not have any freedom unless their owners freed them. These freed slaves were called freedmen and the smarter ones became successful in their chosen professions. Some emperors freed the slaves who had talent and made them their personal assistants. These men became very powerful and rich.

My Humble Home

The homes of the rich were luxurious places and often noblemen had a mansion in Rome and a villa in their country estate. Some of the villas have survived and give us an idea of their lives. The homes made of marble and brick with mosaic flooring were decorated with frescoes on the walls and many sculptures. The wood furniture was embellished with ivory, gold and bronze and leopard skins were used as carpets. The sitting room called the atrium had an opening on the roof and a pool in the centre. In contrast, the poor lived in tiny rooms in tall and badly built apartments and had only some beds and tables. Many of these apartments did not have kitchens so they had to buy their food from food shops. If you were rich, life was very good in Rome.

Dinner Time, Folks!

Most people had bread or biscuits for breakfast and a simple lunch of eggs, cheese or fruit. Dinner was the most important meal of the day with many vegetables and meat dishes. They did not have dining tables and chairs; instead, people lay on couches, reclining on cushions and reached out to the food placed before them on tables. They ate straight from the serving dish, at times using spoons or knives but forks were not known. In those days, common vegetables or fruits like potatoes, tomatoes or chocolates were unknown as these would be brought from South America many centuries later. So there was no course of spaghetti in tomato sauce or chocolate ice cream on the menu.

A Roman banquet would begin in the early evening and go on all night. Men and women ate and drank together. Rich men competed with each other to throw glamorous parties, serving exotic menus. There were some strange dishes

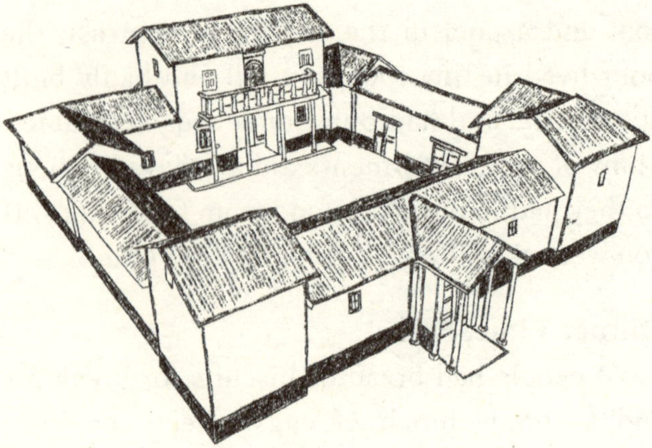

A Roman villa

that were served, like nightingale's tongue, camel's heels and roasted ostrich! They had over two hundred varieties of wines coming from various parts of the empire. The wine was spiced and sweetened with honey and always diluted with water. To drink undiluted wine was not considered very respectable. While up to seven courses were carried in by the slaves, singers, dancers, acrobats and magicians entertained the guests. Wine would flow and people would get quite drunk!

Tunics and Togas

Coming to clothes, the wealthy men wore a complicated dress called toga. This was a huge piece of cloth even longer than a sari and it had to be draped around the body over a long tunic.

It was pleated across the shoulders and was so uncomfortable that men only wore it on formal occasions. Usually men wore a knee-length tunic with a cloak on top, pretty much like the Greeks. Trousers were considered un-manly. Most of their clothes were made of linen or wool as cotton and silk imported from India and China were expensive.

Women wore a long robe called stola and draped a shawl over it called palla. The most expensive pallas were made of dyed muslin from India and silk from China. These textiles travelled across Asia to Rome on the Silk Road. For many centuries, Rome was a huge market for Indian products like cotton, spices, metal ware and pottery.

Women made tall curly hairdos like beehives on their heads and as it was fashionable to look pale, they would whiten their faces with powdered chalk, darken their eyebrows with ash and redden their lips red with plant dye. They did not use soap; instead they would massage oil on the skin and then scrape it off with metal instruments called strigils. Powdered rose petals

were used as a perfume and they used a face cream made from crushed snails.

Gladiators and Games

The emperors were always afraid that the poor would rise in rebellion against them, so they held bloodthirsty shows in open-air stadiums called The Games to keep them entertained. The biggest stadium was the Coliseum in Rome that still stands today, though in ruins. There were armed battles between fighters called gladiators and wild beast hunts. It was all very cruel and disgusting as thousands of animals and hundreds of men were killed while the crowds yelled and cheered. The gladiators fought to death, fighting

with swords, spears and shields. One group of gladiators called retiarus used rather unusual weapons—a huge net and a trident. Most gladiators were slaves, criminals or prisoners of war and a few women also fought at the games.

We think of gladiators as heroes when in fact their lives were very tragic. They were kept imprisoned and had to go through very tough training and then forced to fight. As they entered the arena, they would salute the emperor saying, 'We, who are about to die, salute you!' At times an injured fighter would appeal for mercy and if the emperor raised his thumb, he would be freed. Successful gladiators who survived many battles were freed and became rich and famous like today's rock stars. Graffiti has been found in Pompeii in praise of a local heart-throb named Celadus but most of them died fighting.

No Clowns at This Circus

The racetrack was called the Circus and chariot races would be held here. The largest one in Rome was called the Circus Maximus and it could hold 250,000 people, making it larger than any modern sports stadium. Here men and women were allowed to sit together and the poet Ovid commented that it was a great place to find a girlfriend or boyfriend!

Four teams named after the colours red, blue, yellow and green would compete. The chariots would race around the stadium seven times and people laid bets on them. The wooden chariots were pulled by two or four horses and the races were pretty hair-raising with chariots crashing into each other and toppling over. The drivers wore helmets and carried a small dagger to cut away the leather reins in case they crashed and got dragged away by the panicking horses. The drivers who won led very glamorous lives but it was a dangerous profession and most of them died young in accidents on the racetrack.

Gods Go Roman

Many of the Roman gods and goddesses were in fact Greek, they just changed the names! The Greek king of the gods Zeus became Jupiter;

Poseidon, the god of the sea, became Neptune; and Aphrodite the goddess of love and beauty became Venus. Then to make things more confusing, Apollo the Greek sun god remained Apollo and some new gods and goddesses were created like Flora the goddess of nature.

Huge marble temples were built. There were priests and priestesses; and many festivals were celebrated. Some of the emperors were even declared gods after they died. Both Augustus and his wife Livia became deities and the Roman pantheon kept growing. Emperor Caligula who was quite mad decided he was Jupiter and wandered around carrying a metal thunderbolt to scare people!

Call Me Ceasar

European kings were fascinated by Roman emperors who were called Caesars and tried to create a connection with the Roman Empire even when there was none! In 800 CE Charlemagne king of the Franks crowned himself Emperor of the Romans. In 955 CE, King Otto of Germany declared himself as the Holy Roman Emperor. The German kings called themselves Kaiser and the King of Russia was the Czar—both based on the title Caesar. The Roman crown of victory was made of laurel leaves and Napoleon Bonaparte got himself painted wearing a crown of gold laurel leaves.

Fall of the Empire

For centuries, the Roman Empire ruled supreme but by the 2nd century CE it began to crumble. There were attacks by invaders like German tribes called the Visigoths. The Hun conqueror Atilla swept in from Asia and robbed and killed wherever he went. One incompetent emperor followed another and many were murdered. For example, there were twenty emperors in just fifty years between 235 CE and 284 CE and then the empire broke in two. Finally in 305 CE, the emperor Constantine managed to unite the two halves but he decided to leave Rome because it was being attacked frequently. He shifted his capital eastward to Byzantium that now lies in modern Turkey.

Here he built a new capital that he named after himself and called it Constantinople and with this, the glorious days of Rome were over. Interestingly, like Rome, Constantinople was also built on seven hills. Today, Constantinople is called Istanbul and it is one of Turkey's largest cities. As Rome sank into anarchy, there emerged a new power in Europe based in Constantinople called the Byzantine Empire.

REMARKABLE ROME

- When laying siege to a fort, the Roman army used war machines like giant wooden catapults that threw large rocks, a wooden ram to smash open gates and tall assault towers to climb over high city walls.
- The Byzantine Empire survived till 1453 CE when it was conquered by the Turks who founded the Ottoman Empire.
- Out of the twenty-six letters of the English alphabet, twenty-two come from the Latin alphabet. The Latin alphabet did not have the letters W and Y. For the letters I and J, they wrote I. For U and V, they wrote V.
- Here is a guide to Roman numbers: 1-I. 2-II. 3-III. 4-IV. 5-V. 6-VI. 7-VII. 8-VIII. 9-IX. 10-X. 20-XX. 50-L. 75-LXXV. 100-C. 500-D. 1000-M. 2000-MM. Now try and write today's date!
- The word 'mile' comes from the Latin 'mille', meaning one thousand steps.
- William Shakespeare wrote three plays on the Roman Empire: *Julius Caesar*, *Antony and Cleopatra* and *Coriolanus*.
- Purple was the royal colour. Senators wore a dress called toga with a purple border and only the emperor was allowed to wear a purple toga.

- The Roman soldier carried a 40 kg pack and covered 30 km a day. He wore a clock and carried a leather water bottle, food rations, a shovel, tool kit, dish and pan, a sword, dagger and a javelin.
- There were four kinds of gladiators using different weapons. The Samnite used a sword, a shield and a helmet. The Thracian used a curved dagger and a small metal shield. The Retiarius used a large net and a trident. The Murmillo used a short sword, a huge shield and his helmet was crowned with a fish.
- At performances of plays, women were not allowed to sit in the front row because the men claimed they would run away with the actors. Actually, they just wanted the best seats for themselves.
- During Roman banquets, men were supposed to belch loudly to show their appreciation and even take food home.
- Many stories set in the Roman Empire have been made into Hollywood films. There was the story of a slave rebellion led by a gladiator called *Spartacus*. Elizabeth Taylor played Cleopatra in the 1963 movie by the same name. The film *Ben Hur* has an exciting chariot race.

THE AMERICAS

MAYA, AZTEC, INCA

(1200 BCE–1500 CE)

Far, far away from Asia and Europe a varied group of civilizations were developing in continents that the rest of the world did not even know existed. Till Christopher Columbus voyaged into a strange land in 1492 CE, people were not aware that with Africa, Asia and Europe there existed two more continents. These came to be named North and South America. The Maya, Aztec and Incas were the first civilizations in these two continents.

The civilizations that developed in the Americas were the youngest in the world and flourished at a time when Mesopotamia, Egypt and the Indus Valley had vanished centuries ago. Also, as they were isolated from the rest of the world, their stories are in many ways very different from the others. With the Maya, Aztec and Incas, we enter a unique and wonderfully colourful world of the people of the Americas that Columbus mistakenly called 'India'.

In the New World

The Maya, Aztec and Inca flourished in Central and South America. There were also the other tribes like the Olmecs and the Toltecs. The Maya ruled in the Central American region of south Mexico, Honduras and Guatemala. The Aztecs took over from them and extended their rule over north Mexico. The Inca Empire was in South America, had its capital Cuzco in Peru and included Ecuador, Columbia, Bolivia and parts of Chile and Argentina. The American civilizations

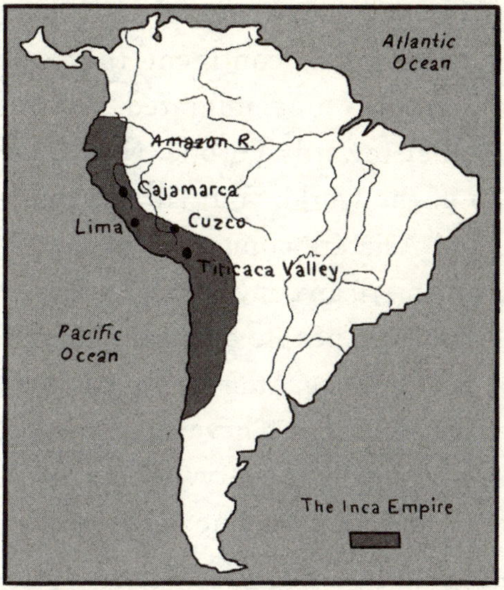

grew between the 4th and 15th centuries CE and built great stone cities. They were the last of the ancient civilizations of the world. Compared to Egypt, India or China that go back to over 5000 years, these are truly the youngest civilizations in the world. Just to give you an idea of the time, when these civilizations were rising, in India the sultans were ruling in Delhi, the Roman Empire had vanished and in China the Ming Dynasty was in power.

Is That Alaska?

It was quite a trek for the Homo sapiens to reach the Americas. They began their journey from Africa and moved north and then at the edge of the African continent they separated into two groups—one migrated towards Asia and the other towards Europe. Now if you look at a map of the world, you will see that Africa, Europe and Asia are connected by land but not to the two American continents. So there was no way the nomadic people could have crossed the huge expanse of the Atlantic or Pacific oceans to reach the Americas. They were simple hunter-gatherers who *walked* everywhere; they did not have ships; and definitely no aeroplanes! So how did they land in the Americas?

It is actually a climate-change story. This was the time of the Ice Age and the seas were frozen into glaciers in the North Pole. This meant that the level of the seawater was much lower and that had revealed a patch of land that connected north-east Asia, around Siberia, to the Alaska region of North America. For thousands of years there was a slow migration of people into Alaska. Later, when the Ice Age ended and the glaciers began to melt, the water levels rose and covered this land bridge. Today this sea is called the Bering Strait and you can only visit it by ship.

These intrepid adventurers searching for food moved southward from Alaska through Canada and the United States, then down to Mexico, entering South America through Peru, Argentina, Chile...and very, very slowly they covered both the continents. Then they developed agriculture, built cities, fought wars, made pottery and jewellery—and we got the oldest civilizations of the Americas.

The Olmecs Came First

The Mexico region saw a number of tribes who were the first to build cities. The tropical forests of Mexico and Guatemala have the ruins of many. Like Greece, this region had city states with their own political systems, culture and religions. The royal family, priests and nobility lived in the cities while close to 90 per cent of the population, mostly of farmers and craftsmen, lived in the countryside.

The oldest city builders were a tribe called the Olmecs who lived in west Mexico. They built very rough pyramids with earth instead of stone and carved huge stone heads of men with

a very grim expression, droopy lips and angry eyes. Some of these stone heads were three metres high but they were not attached to any bodies and we don't know if they were images of gods. The Olmecs had a system of writing but we know very little about them. However, many Olmec traditions were carried on by later tribes.

Tongue-Twister Names

The Mayans and Aztecs built cities with pyramids in the centre where they worshipped their gods. What we would like to know is why did they give such impossible names to their cities and gods? They are harder to pronounce than the Egyptian ones. The Aztec capital was called Tenochtitlan while other cities were called Itzapalapa, Yucatan, Chapultepec and Coyoacan. Tenochtitlan was on the site of the modern Mexican capital, Mexico City.

Their gods included the plumed serpent called Quetzalcoatl, another called Tezcatlipoca, the god of the mirror, and Mictlantecuhtli, the god of war. With such teeth-gnashing titles, it must have taken them ages to say their prayers. And no wonder they never developed an alphabet—imagine trying to spell them all correctly! The Maya and Aztec used a pictorial or hieroglyphic script. Three Aztec books have survived, though in a very fragile condition, and the rest were destroyed by the Spanish. Scholars have now succeeded in deciphering these scripts

Tlaloc,
God of Rain

Huitzilopochtli,
God of War and Sun

Quetzalcoatl, God of
Civilization and Order

Tezcatlipoca, God of
Destiny and Good Fortune

Xochiquetzal, Goddess
of Fertility and Art

Tepeyallotl, God of
Earthquakes, Echoes
and Jaguars

Xolotl, God of Fire,
Lightning and Death

Mictlantecuhtli,
God of Death

and we know quite a lot about the Aztec people and their religion.

Bloodthirsty Gods

The Maya and Aztec believed that the only way to keep their gods happy and make sure the sun rose the next day was by constantly offering them human beings as sacrifice. Soon it became a civilization that was obsessed with death and mummification and they even celebrated a feast of the dead. Usually, the victims were prisoners of war or men kidnapped from other tribes who were killed by the priests over a sacrificial stone on top of the pyramids. In the ceremony the heart of the victim was cut out, the body thrown to the ground and the skin was worn by the priest as they danced.

To understand just how bloodthirsty they were, try to imagine this utterly gory scene: to mark the opening of a temple in 1485 CE at Tenochtitlan, 20,000 captives were sacrificed and then their hearts were burnt in a stone bowl.

Pyramid Builders

The Maya and Aztec built their temples as pyramids, which started a theory among historians that somehow the Egyptians had landed there. Don't you believe it! These pyramids were very different—mounds of packed earth covered with a stone facade while the Egyptians built them all in stone, which required a lot of expertise. Also, the Egyptian pyramids had smooth sides, and as they were the tombs for kings, there was a burial chamber in the centre. The Aztec pyramids had stepped sides so that you could climb up with a platform on top where there was a temple and the sacrifices were held. Historians say that these American civilizations

were completely isolated from the rest of the world and knew nothing of Egypt. This led to another crazy theory that the pyramids were built by aliens!

The Mayans built the first pyramid temples around 300 BCE at the city of Tikal in Guatemala. People had to climb hundreds of steep steps to reach the top. The El Mirador temple complex was huge and covered over 16 square kilometres. The Mayans built the city called Teotihuacan around 50 CE and laid the streets in straight lines. In the centre was the temple to the Sun God that they worshipped and over 200,000 people lived there.

The King and His People

Only the king, priests, noblemen, officials and their servants lived in the cities. The rest of the population were farmers and craftsmen who lived in the countryside. They supplied the city with food and textiles and pottery. Only the priests were allowed on top of the pyramids where they performed their gristly duties. The Aztec settled by the bank of Lake Texcoco in 1325 CE and built the city of Tenochtitlan on an island in the lake, connected to the mainland by three causeways with wooden drawbridges. In the centre was the sacred precinct with pyramid-temples. Here there were two shrines—to Huitzilopochtli, the god of war and sun, and Tlaloc, the god of rain and harvests.

The Aztec king was supposed to have been chosen by the gods and so no one was allowed to look at his face. People had to stand before him with their head bent. He was carried everywhere on a palanquin and when he stepped on the ground, carpets were laid on it. In contrast, ordinary people led simple lives and there were a lot of rules in this civilization. For example, women could only wear a wraparound skirt and a tunic in a very simple design and the men wore a loin cloth and a cape

on top. This cape could only reach down to the knees and if you wore one that reached down to the ankles, you would be sentenced to death! The rich of course wore colourful clothes, at times decorated with bright feathers.

The Aztec life was harsh, brutal and centred on war. All the men had to fight in the army and their main job was to collect tributes and capture prisoners who could then be sacrificed to their bloodthirsty gods. Ultimately, this endless cruelty brought their rule to an end as it made them very unpopular with their subject tribes. These tribes welcomed the arrival of the Spanish conquistadors and helped them defeat the Aztec.

A Very Interesting Calendar

The Aztec counted in fives and wrote them down in dots and dashes. So 1 was one dot, 2 was two dots, then 5 was a dash and 6 a dash with a dot on top. They did know about the zero and it was drawn as a shell. Try to write today's date in dots and dashes and you will find it taking up a lot of space! The Aztec astronomers developed a detailed calendar and studied the stars carefully. The Maya calendar had predicted that the world would end on 22 December 2012 and on that day many around the world held their breath, but nothing happened!

The Mayans even worked out the times of the eclipse of the sun and moon and their calendar was more accurate than the ones used in Europe at that time. For example, they calculated the cycle of the planet Venus going around the sun at 584 days and got it wrong by just two hours. Their calendar had twenty months of twenty days each and the months were named after nature and wildlife like crocodile, monkey, jaguar, rain, flower or water and each month had a pictorial symbol.

A Basket of Plenty

Every time you have a chilly or capsicum, you should thank the Aztec. The Aztec and Incas have given the world an overflowing cornucopia of fruits and vegetables that we eat every day. Can you imagine a life without potatoes that the Incas gifted the world? Even today they grow 200 varieties of potatoes and the word 'potato' comes from the Inca word 'batata' for sweet potato. Surprisingly, in Maharashtra, they call potatoes 'batata'—looks like the Marathis met someone from Peru while frying their batata vadas!

Many of these foods were carried to India by the Portuguese who had colonies in South America. Among the other American foods introduced by the Portuguese are corn, cashew nuts, peanuts, pineapple, capsicum, tomato, cocoa beans and of course our super-hot green chilly! It is hard to imagine, but when King Ashoka had a dal with tadka or King Akbar tasted a Mughlai korma it was spiced with pepper and not chilly.

The Aztec had an unusual system of growing crops. As there was very little fertile land, Aztec farmers grew their crops on artificial islands built on lakes. They floated layers of woven material on the water, on which they put layers of earth and grew vegetables on them. So every morning the farmers would take their boats to the floating fields called chinampas to tend to their crops. The main grain was corn that was ground and made into tortillas and tamales like they do even today in Mexico. The Aztec also brewed beer from corn and the Inca loved to eat guinea pigs!

An Aztec poem

No one comes on this earth to stay
Our bodies are like rose trees
They grow petals and then wither and die
But our hearts are like grass in springtime
They live on and forever grow green again.

Gold, Beads and Feathers

The Aztec were great architects and craftsmen and the amazing thing is that they managed to build pyramids when they did not have iron tools or know the use of the wheel! Their potters made pottery by hand even as late as the 15th century. They used stone hammers and chisels and even their swords had stone blades. They knew the use of gold and silver, and the metals were moulded to make beautiful ornaments and masks. The nobility loved elaborate headdresses, fans, capes and shields all decorated with colourful feathers with gold, silver and gemstones on its borders. As you may have noticed with Native Indians, feathered headdresses were very important to the Mesoamericans, and the craftsmen who made these plumed headdresses were called amantakas.

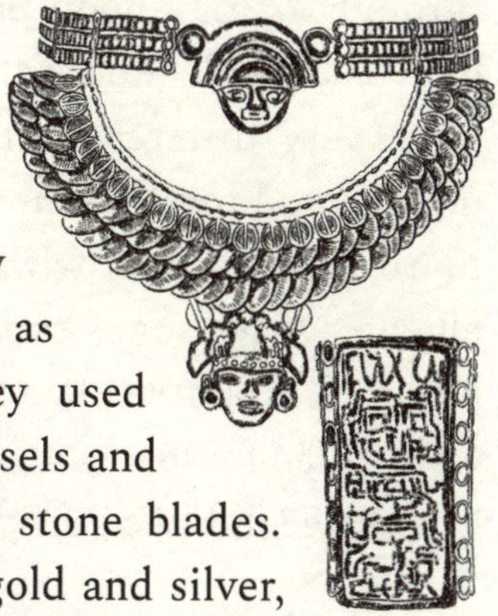

The Sacred Ball Game

All the Aztec cities had a ball court built near the temple to play a game called pok-a-tok and historians think it was somehow a religious game. They used a solid rubber ball with rubber extracted from native trees. The ball was bounced off the high walls and the players tried to drop it through a stone hoop placed on a wall. Sounds like basketball, doesn't it? However, the rules were very different because the players were not allowed to use their hands or feet. They had to control the ball with their hips, thighs and elbows. Also, some carvings show ball players being decapitated. Did that mean that players were killed for losing at a ball game? Who knows! The Aztec did like sacrificing human beings...

The Mighty Incas

Legends say that the Inca Empire was founded by a god named Manco Capac and his sister Mama Oello, who were supposed to be the children of the sun. The sun was the main god of the Incas and they were the first rulers in the region of Peru. The real builder of the Inca Empire was a king called Pachacuti who ruled in the 15th century CE in the Peru region and conquered many neighbouring areas. His son Topa built the city of Quito, the capital of modern Peru. At the height of their power, the Inca Empire covered 4000 kilometres from north to south along the Pacific Ocean, from Ecuador to Chile, making it as large as the Roman Empire.

What is amazing is that the Incas had no written script. They had a well-structured administration, a network of roads and an efficient way of collecting taxes and managed to successfully control such a large area without written records. The Incas became famous across the world for their legendary wealth, especially for their gold. The name of the empire came from their king's title—Sapa Inca or Supreme Inca. The most important deity in the Inca pantheon was Inti, the sun god, and the Sapa Inca was worshipped as the son of Inti. The Sapa Inca had many queens but his senior-most queen was always his sister. They were so rich that each new king built his own palace while the body of the dead king was mummified and kept in his old home and regularly taken out in procession.

Dots, Dashes and Knots

The Incas calculated numbers by tying knots on a length of string called quipu. The cords were of various thickness and colours and numbers and data were marked by knots of various sizes and positions on the string. The quipus were sent from one city to another, carried by a relay of runners just like letters were sent in other countries. There were special officials who knew how to tie and interpret the knots called

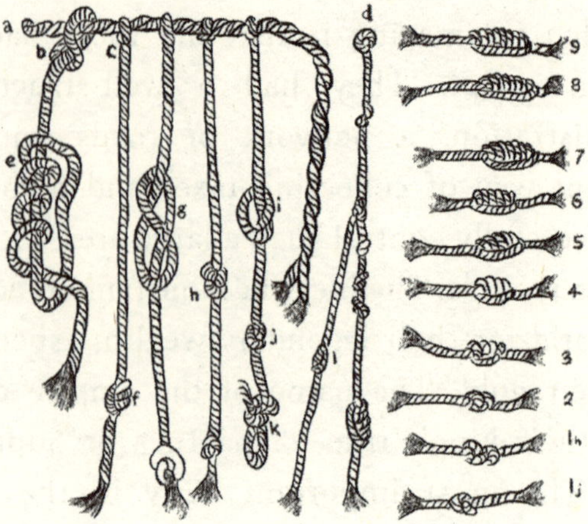

quipu camayocs and in this way they kept track of everything from population, goods, herds of cattle and taxes. The problem is that no one can read the quipu knots anymore. And that this meant they had no poetry, stories or written history.

Inti, the Sun God

The most powerful Inca god was Inti followed by Mamaquilla, the moon goddess, and Pachamama, mother earth. Inti was worshipped as the giver of life and huge discs made of solid gold were kept in the temples. It is very similar to the worship of Ra in Egypt. They called gold the 'sweat of the sun' and silver the 'tears of the moon'. They had such rich gold and silver mines that at their biggest temple they had a garden made of gold and silver trees. In medieval Europe, this started the rumour of El Dorado, a mythical Inca city made of gold. In fact, El Dorado was a legendary Inca chief who used to cover his body with gold dust so that he could glow like the sun.

Inti, the sun god

Moral Precepts

The Incas had three precepts:

Ama sua: Do not steal

Ama ilulla: Do not lie

Ama quella: Do not be lazy

Living in the Inca World

The Incas grew vegetables that would change the food habits of the world when the Spanish and Portuguese colonized the region and introduced these vegetables to Europe and their colonies in Asia. The highlands of the Andes mountain ranges produced vegetables that the world had never seen. Can you imagine meals without potatoes? The Inca grew 200 varieties of potatoes on fields carved into hillsides but surprisingly they did not know the use of the plough. The cereal quinoa that has become popular as a health food recently is also a gift of Peru. They grew coca leaves that people chewed to give themselves energy and control hunger.

Cusco, the capital of the Inca Empire, was a well run and clean city because they had officers ensuring that homes were kept clean. Clear water channels ran through the streets bringing fresh drinking water from the hills. The Incas built simple houses and palaces and did not know how to build an arch. They also did not have many carvings unlike the Maya and Aztec. Machu Picchu, in the Andes Mountains, is the best preserved city of the Inca Empire. Here the temples, palaces and houses were built of granite blocks fitted closely together without the use of mortar. After the region was conquered by Spain, it was forgotten till it was discovered again in 1911 by Hiram Bingham of the United States.

The Inca Empire was in a very hilly area and because they were not aware of the use of the

The city of Machu Picchu

wheel, llamas were used to carry goods along high mountain roads. The people used the llama as a pack animal and also for meat. There were also tiny camels like the alpaca and vicuna that were herded for their wool. People led simple lives and it was only the royal family that had palaces. As there was no written script, there was no system of education, so children did not have to go to school either.

The Spanish Conquest

For centuries, the Silk Road had brought goods to Italy which dominated international trade.

In the 15th century, other European countries began to look for new routes to trade with Asia, especially with Indonesia, China and India. The first kingdoms to send ships were Spain and Portugal. The Portuguese sailed east and Vasco da Gama arrived on the coast of Kerala in 1498 CE. The Spanish headed west when Queen Isabella sponsored a navigator called Christopher Columbus, from Genoa in Italy. He was also trying to find a route to India, unaware that an unknown continent blocked his way. In 1492 CE, he landed on the West Indies islands in the Caribbean and thought he had found India. The joke is that he made three more voyages and never realized his mistake!

The arrival of the Spanish adventurers called conquistadors, searching for treasures, ended the great American civilizations. There had been many stories of how the Incas had gold and shiploads of adventurers headed to the new world in search of a legendary land called El Dorado or the kingdom of the 'Golden Man'. Of course, the stories were great exaggerations and very few men made any money. Hernan Cortes (1484–1547) who destroyed the Aztec Empire died in poverty and Francisco Pizarro (1475–1541) who ruined the Inca Empire was murdered.

Their big advantage was that they had swords, guns and horses. Hernan Cortes came with just 600 soldiers and then was helped by the other tribes who were angry at losing men in sacrifices by the Aztec. The Aztec king Montezuma welcomed Cortes because he thought the fair-skinned and bearded Spanish soldier riding a horse was their god Quetzalcoatl. It was a big mistake because the Spanish looted the empire and so much silver was sent back to Europe that the price of the metal crashed. Also, a lot of the treasures were robbed along the way by sea pirates.

Another conquistador named Francisco Pizarro headed for South America and conquered the Incas. He had just sixty-three horsemen and 200 foot-soldiers. He succeeded because he arrived at a time when there were two claimants to the Inca throne and a civil war was raging. Pizarro and his guns proved superior to the Inca warriors.

The Europeans also brought diseases like small pox and tuberculosis that killed thousands of native Indians because they had no immunity. Soon the people had been colonized and were forced to work in plantations and treated like slaves. At its height, the Spanish Empire in the

Americas spread from California to Chile and was bigger than the British Empire.

AWESOME AMERICAS

- It was the Italian explorer Amerigo Vespucci who landed in South America in 1499 and realized that it was a new continent. A 1507 map of the new world named the continents of America after him.
- Christopher Columbus brought the first pineapple to Europe and soon potatoes, tomatoes and other vegetables followed and completely changed European cuisine. Imagine trying to make pasta without tomato sauce!
- The Aztec called themselves 'Mexica' and 'Tenochca'. They originally came from a place called Aztlan, 'place of the herons'.
- In the 1500s, when the Aztec city of Tenochtitlan had a population of 3,00,000 people, it was much bigger than European cities. For example, Toledo the capital of Spain had just 18,000 people living there.
- The Aztec soldiers were called eagle or jaguar warriors and wore jaguar skins and elaborate headdresses set with feathers.

- The Aztec grew cocoa but did not drink hot chocolate or make it into a chocolate bar. Cocoa beans were so precious, they were often used as money. The idea of adding sugar to cocoa to make a sweet drink began in Europe.
- The Aztec made a drink from the leaves of a cactus called agave. They used the thorns as needles to make ropes, clothes and sandals with the fibres. Agave is still brewed in Mexico.
- The Aztec were obsessed with death and their god of death had a grinning skull for a face. They made masks out of human skulls encrusted with turquoise and sea-shells and lined with red leather.
- Mexico City has two metro stations named after Aztec kings—Moctezuma and Cuauhtemoc.
- Food names like chocolate, tomato, chilli, avocado, tamale, taco and chipotle come from the Aztec language called Nahuatl. The salad salsa is an Inca word.

AFRICA

A FORGOTTEN CONTINENT

(500 BCE–1500 CE)

Sometimes history moves in very strange ways. Take the continent of Africa which is, after Asia, the largest and most populous continent in the world. It is crucial to the story of human beings because Africa was the birthplace of the human race as the first Homo sapiens appeared

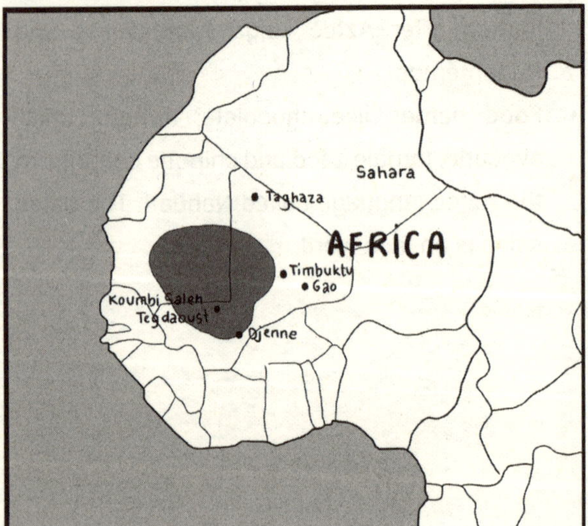

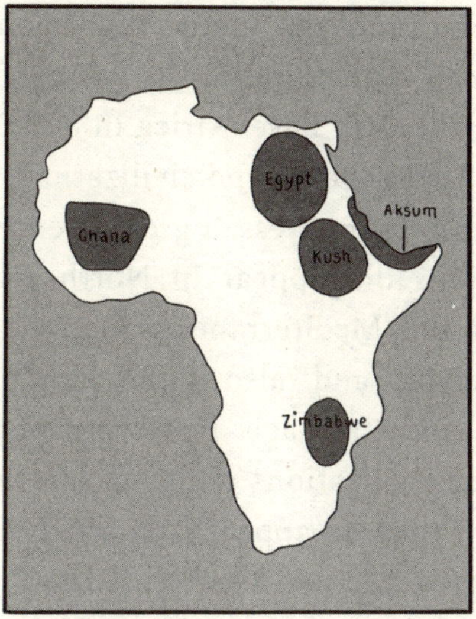

here. We know the history of North Africa, most importantly Egypt and also Morocco, Algeria, Tunisia and Libya but the interior of the continent vanishes from the pages of history for centuries. So, when it comes to the story of ancient civilizations, Africa is the forgotten continent. It is even more puzzling because it is from the savannahs of central Africa that Homo sapiens began their journey.

Civilization is the story of human ingenuity and it begins with the simple stone-cutting tools like the hand axe. The archaeologist Louis Leakey found the oldest chopping tool at the Olduvai Gorge in Tanzania in 1931, dated to 1.8

to 2 million years ago and it proved conclusively that human culture began in Africa. This also proves that we all have 'Africa in our DNA' and without Africa there is no civilization. After the initial surge of progress, a great silence follows. Civilizations did appear in North Africa that bordered the Mediterranean Sea, the greatest being Egypt, and also later kingdoms like Morocco and Carthage. However, we have few records of civilizations rising in interior Africa and when they do appear it is much later than China or Greece and closer to the time of the Aztecs and Incas. It is as if the Homo sapiens walked away and forgot their homeland.

The Landscape of Africa

Africa is not a small area; it is a continent and three times the size of the United States of America. It has a landscape that spans from the tropical forests of Congo and Ghana to the valleys of great rivers like the Nile, Niger, Congo, Zambezi, the Blue and White Nile. There are verdant grasslands and the endless arid expanse of the Sahara Desert. However, except for Egypt and some if its neighbouring kingdoms, we know very little about the history of Africa. There are oral accounts of kings and battles but we know hardly anything about the life of the people, its culture and technological progress. There are few buildings, carvings, paintings and, crucially, very little that has been put down in writing.

Agriculture developed in the Nile valley but it did not spread to interior Africa, probably because of the difficult terrain. From Egypt, agriculture moved south into Sudan and Ethiopia but the rest of Africa would take the first step towards civilization centuries later. Another factor may have been the appearance of the Sahara desert—another story of climate change. It is hard to imagine but at one time the Sahara was a green, forested land where hippos and rhinos roamed and not camels. Today, it is the fastest spreading desert in the world and all its rivers have vanished. This must have impacted the lives of the people of the region and its history.

We know that around 6000 BCE the Sahara had rivers and forests because there are rock paintings in caves that show men in canoes hunting hippopotamus in a river and even drawings of elephants! Today, only Arab nomads cross the endless sand dunes on camels and wander from oasis to oasis. At one time, farmers in the Sahara grew crops like millet, sorghum and yams but then the climate changed as the rains moved away and the area began to dry around

3500 BCE. Some historians feel this climate change may be the reason that civilizations did not rise in the region. After all, if you could not grow crops how could you have villages and cities?

Many Stories But No Books

What is very puzzling is why most Africans, like the Incas of South America, did not develop a script and learn to read and write. History was passed on orally through storytelling but as there are no written records a lot has been lost. When trying to gather the history of Africa, archaeologists have to depend on these oral traditions and the artefacts they find during their excavations. As there is no literature, we have none of the interesting details of how the people lived, their religion and culture. In the memories of balladeers what was preserved were the stories of kings and battles. No one told stories of clothes and festivals, recipes and music, all those little things that really create a civilization.

It is the records kept by officials that preserve the history of a people but as there was no literacy there were no scribes or mandarin officials and no written laws as these kingdoms were run by a royal family and their tribe. We have to thank the Arab traders for whatever we know about these 'dim and shadowy kingdoms'. The first records of West African kingdoms were kept by Arab traders after the 8th century CE by when the Egyptian civilization was 3000 years old! This shows just how little we know of old African kingdoms like Kush or Mali that were trading with the world but did not have a written language.

Somehow the belief grew that there were no African civilizations except Egypt. For instance, when the outstanding sculptures of Nigeria—what are called the Ife heads—were discovered, many Europeans refused to believe this magnificent art was African in origin. Some even said that Greek sculptors had landed in Nigeria and had made them. When the citadel of Great Zimbabwe was discovered, some declared that people from Israel came to build it.

There is no great architecture like the pyramids of Egypt or a cultural heritage like the development of agriculture and the first script of Mesopotamia. There were no great inventions like those in China or political philosophy that developed in Greece. Even the more primitive civilizations like the Aztec and Inca that developed later have much more to offer. For us, Africa remains the Dark Continent but with the work of historians and archaeologists it is now slowly appearing into the light.

Civilizations in Eastern Africa

The first civilization to rise in Africa was Egypt and its influence spread along the Nile as agriculture spread south to modern Sudan and Ethiopia. Here, kingdoms like Nubia, Kush and Aksum rose around the port cities on the Red Sea and along the coast of the Indian Ocean. These were smaller kingdoms with simpler cultures that were overshadowed by the glitter of Egypt that dominated the region.

It is on the wall paintings of Egyptian tombs that we first discover images of the people of Nubia. Among all the gorgeous paintings of pharaohs and queens, dancers and noblemen, the Nubians with their ebony skin and African features are easy to spot. They are shown bringing tributes to the pharaoh: rows of dusky-skinned men in white garments bearing gifts of crops and fruits, jewellery, furs and exotic animals like monkeys.

A Nubian citizen

Ancient Nubia

Nubia's history can be traced back to 2500 BCE. The stories of great east African kingdoms of Nubia and Kush have somehow got lost behind the dazzle of the Egyptian cities like Luxor and Thebes. In fact, the cities of Nubia and then Kush flourished for over a thousand years, reaching their peak around 1000 BCE. Nubia grew along the fertile land by the banks of the River Nile, south of Egypt in the region of modern Sudan. It was the first region in Central Africa to develop agriculture. Nubia became very wealthy through its trade with Egyptian kingdoms and imitating the pharaohs, the kings and nobility of Nubia built elaborate tombs. It was when Egypt's Pharaoh Thutmose I conquered Nubia around 1500 BCE that the Nubians arrived at the pharaoh's court in Luxor bearing tribute.

Here Comes Kush

By 2000 BCE, Nubia was called the Kingdom of Kush in the records of the Egyptians and it covered the region of southern Egypt and Sudan. The Kushites had one great advantage over the Egyptians: they were the first to make iron tools and that improved agriculture, crafts and also helped produced better weapons. Kush had ports on the Indian Ocean and traded in ivory, incense, gold and iron not just with Egypt but also by sea with Asia and became both a trading partner and also a rival of Egypt.

The kings of Kush did not want to continue sending tribute to Egypt and in 724 BCE, King Piye (also known as Piankhi) invaded and occupied Luxor, the capital of Egypt. Kush had thus conquered the largest empire in the world and they ruled as the 25th Dynasty of Egypt. Then the Assyrians invaded from the north and defeated Kush. The Kushites withdrew into their

The kingdom of Kush

own land till 500 BCE when they were invaded and conquered by a kingdom called Aksum.

Kush adopted many Egyptian customs and had a tradition of powerful queen-mothers called Candace who ruled beside their sons like the Egyptian female pharaohs.

They worshipped Egyptian gods and goddesses like Ammon and Isis and also mummified their dead. In the 4th century BCE, Kush had a language called Meroitic and a script that was written with a stylus and carved on stone. These carvings are all we have to give us the history of the kingdom and sadly all you get are a list of kings and the battles they fought. The kings built their tombs as pyramids but these looked a little different from the Egyptian ones;

Candace, the queen-mother of the kingdom

they were much smaller and shaped differently. As a matter of fact, today the region around Khartoum in Sudan has more pyramids than all of Egypt.

Where Is Punt?

Egyptian records mention trading with a kingdom called Punt but historians cannot find its exact location. Egyptians called it the 'Land of the Gods'. It was rich in ebony, gold, a rare incense called myrrh and exotic animals like apes and leopards. The great female pharaoh Queen Hatshepsut sent a trading mission to Punt and it was obviously a very important event because it is mentioned in all her records. The mission was a flotilla of boats carrying Egyptian goods that brought back many rare and precious things. Some historians think that maybe Punt was in fact Nubia or Kush.

A Ship to Aksum

The kingdom of Aksum replaced Kush and prospered in modern Ethiopia and Eritrea. This coastal region was a big trading centre for many centuries and had ports where cargo ships from far-off lands like India, Persia and China docked carrying porcelain, spices and textiles and took away ivory, gold, ebony wood and slaves. International trade always makes a region more culturally rich and sophisticated and Aksum had a metropolitan society. Aksum did have a written script known as Ge'ez and after the Egyptian hieroglyphics it was one of the earliest scripts to appear in Africa but very few samples have survived.

Like Nubia and Kush, the people of Aksum worshipped Egyptian gods and built pyramids and carved tall stone columns called obelisks. All this changed in 330 CE when two Christian missionaries were shipwrecked at a port. They preached the gospel and converted King Ezana to Christianity and he made Christianity the state religion. In 1270, King Yekuno Amlak seized the throne declaring that he was a descendant of the Jewish king Solomon and his consort the Queen of Sheba. He claimed that their son founded the kingdom of Aksum. The last emperor of Ethiopia Haile Selassie (1930–74) was a direct descendant of Yekuno Amlak and he was worshipped by a sect called Rastafarians in far off Jamaica as a messiah.

Worshipping a King

The Rastafarians are found in the Caribbean Island of Jamaica and they are easy to spot because of their extraordinary hair, all curly dreadlocks, usually worn by the men. What is fascinating is that the members of this religious sect that began in the 1930s, worship Haile Selassie, the last emperor of Ethiopia—a country located thousands of miles away in Africa. The Rastas have given us the lovely beat of Reggae music and its most famous singer was Bob Marley.

The Rastas, who are the descendants of African slaves, look back with nostalgia at Africa and at Ethiopia, a country that was never colonized by Europeans. As a reaction to poverty, racism and the pain of colonization, they believe that Haile Selassie was a messiah and an incarnation of god who will save them.

Aksum was the first region in Africa to become Christian and today modern Ethiopia continues to be the oldest Christian country in Africa. By the 7th century CE, most of North and West Africa had converted to Islam and Muslim armies invaded Aksum. The northern part was conquered by the armies of the Ottoman Empire and the southern by the Sennan Sultanate. Aksum shrank into the area of modern Ethiopia and then with Muslim countries in the north blocking access, they lost touch with the rest of the world for 800 years but continued to be a Christian nation. Today Ethiopia follows the Coptic church of Egypt, one of the oldest Christian churches in the world.

First Came the Arabs

Africa's earliest trade with Asia and Europe was through Arab merchants who would introduce Islam to the continent. After the 7th century, the camel caravans of Arabs and the nomads called Berbers crossed 1600 kilometres of the arid Sahara to reach the kingdoms of western Africa

like Ghana and Mali. They were remarkable traders, moving with their camel caravans from oasis to oasis, facing the danger of bandits. They would cover up to 300 kilometres of the sandy landscape in a week trading in salt, gold and later slaves and bringing textiles and leather goods from Asia and Europe.

These merchants from Arabia and the Ottoman Empire traded in slaves much before the Europeans arrived looking for slaves. They called Africa Bilad al-Sudan or the 'land of the black people' while for Africans they were the 'white people'. Many educated Arabs were employed by African kings like Ashanti as officials and they created the first literate civil service. These Muslim clerks and later travellers began to keep records and write the history of the region. Unlike people from the European countries, the Arabs only came to trade and never colonized the region.

Islam came to Africa in the 7th century more through trade with the Caliphate of Damascus than conquest. Damascus was a big trading post on the Silk Road. It is the Arabs who opened the interiors of Africa to the world by travelling across land from Damascus and Byzantium and by sea as far as India and China. They used the astrolabe to navigate the desert and the oceans by marking the position of the stars. Many Arab traders settled in the East African ports and married the local Bantu women and called the local people 'Sawahila' or coast people. Later, the language spoken here came to be known as Swahili. They called the coastal area the land of the Zanzi or Zanzibar. They traded with India for textiles and spices and with China for silk and porcelain. Even today you can find piles of broken porcelain on the beaches of Ethiopia.

Solomon and the Queen of Sheba

The Old Testament of the Bible mentions a queen of the kingdom of Sheba who came to Babylon to meet Solomon, the king of the Jews. No one is sure what her name was or where she came from. Some say she came from the Saba kingdom of Yemen while the Ethiopians claim she was their queen Makeda who led a trade delegation to Israel. The Ethiopians could be right because they seemed to have had contact with the Jews as their language has Semitic words and it is the oldest Christian region in Africa.

Civilizations in Western Africa

Till 1000 BCE, Africa mainly had villages and a primitive culture. They shared a language called Bantu and the only cities were in the ports of eastern Africa in the kingdoms of Nubia, Kush and then Aksum. Most Africans lived in villages governed by a chieftain and a council of elders. Their way of agriculture was to burn the forest, grow crops and then move on when the ground became less fertile—what is called slash and burn cultivation. When you live in a thatched hut, it is easy to move your family and cattle in search of newer land and live as nomads.

The Bantu people kept shifting southward and thus, very gradually, they covered most of Africa. However, as they never settled anywhere long enough to build cities, they never laid the foundation of a civilization. The kingdoms of western Africa appear much later than those in Sudan and Ethiopia and among them the most powerful were Ghana, Mali and Songhay. Later, a mysterious kingdom grew in South Africa called Great Zimbabwe but we know very little about it.

Your Majesty Ghana

Like the pharaohs of Egypt, a dynasty of kings called Ghana appeared in West Africa. This area is called Sub-Saharan Africa as it is south of the great desert. The medieval kingdom stood by the Atlantic Ocean around the modern states of Senegal, Ivory Coast, Burkina Faso and Togo. Agriculture arrived quite late here in the early years of the Christian era and until then the people lived by fishing in the sea and rivers and gathering food from the forests. Then they began to grow sorghum, cassava and bananas. Around 300 CE, the kingdom of Ghana rose through its connections to the Arab traders who crossed the Sahara to trade with it for gold and salt. Ghana covered a vast area of over 2,58,998 square kilometres and grew rich by trade and also by taxation of the trader caravans.

The word Ghana is a title and means 'warrior king' in the Soninke language. It was the Arabs who began to call the kingdom Ghana. The 9th century Berber historian and geographer Al Yaqubi describes Ghana as a highly organized state that practiced religious tolerance as people were Muslims and also believed in the old pagan faith. The contact with the Arab traders meant that gradually the people converted to Islam and the Arabs introduced a script, books and kept a record of the history of the kingdom.

Among the many dynasties that ruled in Ghana was the warrior-like tribe called Ashanti. Ghana is the first civilization in western Africa that we know of and its history has survived mainly because of the Arab traders who kept written records. It was conquered by a Muslim general called Abu Bakr ibn Umar and was replaced by the kingdom of Mali that caught the attention of the world through the wealth of its kings. The Portuguese were the first Europeans to arrive here in the 15th century looking for gold and slaves and soon colonized and impoverished the people.

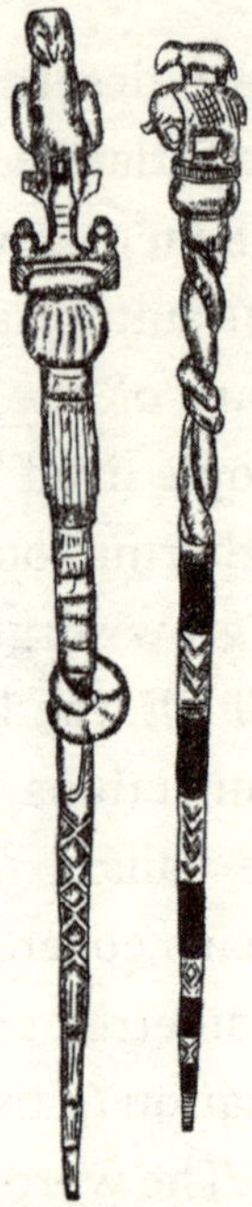

Regalia belonging to the Ashanti tribe

A Golden Audience

The Arab traveller Abu U'bayd al-Bakri, describing a royal audience with the king of Ghana, wrote that he sat in a pavilion ringed by ten horses caparisoned in gold. The pages stood holding golden swords and shields, the princes had their hair plaited in gold and the guard dogs wore gold collars with little bells that jingled.

It's All Gold in Mali

There was a small city state named Mali that was part of the Ghana kingdom, which won independence around 1200 CE. Within a century it conquered much of the territory, and become rich from trade and conquered all of Ghana. Mali was a landlocked kingdom with the Sahara desert in the north and the Niger and Senegal rivers flowing through it. The kingdom was founded by a famous warrior called Sundiate Keita who is said to have been crippled but was still a fierce fighter. For a while Mali was the most powerful kingdom in western Africa but the people of Ghana kept rebelling so it had a tumultuous history. Gradually Mali got broken up into smaller states and vanished from history.

During the time Mali was the richest state in Africa, its largest city Timbuktu was a centre

Mansa Musa, one of the Kings of Mali, as depicted in the Catalan Atlas

of not just trade with busy markets but also of culture and learning. In the large markets of the city they traded in salt, gold, ivory and slaves. The kings of Mali were called Mansa and the greatest ruler was Mansa Musa I who was known for his wealth and piety. He built many mosques, Islamic schools called madrassas and libraries.

Mansa Musa is remembered for his famous pilgrimage to Mecca in 1324 CE that came to be called the 'Pilgrimage of Gold'. The Arab historian Al-Umari wrote that Mansa Musa travelled with a huge entourage of 500 slaves wearing gold, carrying golden staffs and 10,000 horses. During this Haj, he distributed so much gold carried on eighty camels that the price of the precious metal fell in the market. Most interestingly, he came home with a huge collection of Arabic books, set up a library in Timbuktu and welcomed Arabic scholars. He invited Muslim architects to build the great mosque of Timbuktu as he sent ambassadors to Egypt, Morocco and Arabia.

Songhai Comes and Goes

In 1468 CE, the Songhai people conquered Mali and established a new kingdom. Led by the general Sunni Ali, they conquered most of the regions that were once a part of the Ghana and Mali empires. They shifted their capital from

Timbuktu to Gao and the kingdom grew rich by controlling the trade routes where they imposed fees on merchants and also from the gold mines along the Niger River. At its height, the Songhai Empire was larger than Mali. By then the kings of the region were Muslims but many of their subjects still followed the old pagan religions. This led to much conflict that weakened the kings till Songhai was invaded and conquered by the king of Morocco.

Let's Go to Timbuktu!

The modern city of Timbuktu stands beside the Niger River in Morocco. In popular western culture it became a symbol of a remote and

The mud mosque at Timbuktu

strange place. The medieval city was a centre of trade and learning with famous bazaars called souks and colleges called madrassas but it was not all culture and learning. It also had a darker side as the centre of the slave trade and human beings were sold like goods in its markets. Its wealth came from the sorrow of poor, helpless people.

There was a popular saying: 'Salt comes from the north, gold from the south...but the treasures of wisdom come from Timbuktu'. The city's madrassas had mathematicians, astronomers, writers and artists. The famous mosques of Timbuktu were made of earth or adobe and look very different from our idea of mosques with domes and minarets. There was a book trade that was very rare in the region and the Sankore University was famous for its library which had 700,000 manuscripts. In the 13th century, a Moroccan diplomat named Hasan ibn Muhammad travelled to Mali and wrote of his experiences. He was called Leo Africanus by the Europeans and was regarded as an authority on the geography of the area.

Great Zimbabwe

It is not easy to find great kingdoms in the South African region before the arrival of the Europeans in the 16th century. One that is remembered because of an extraordinary city is Great Zimbabwe but all we have are its ghostly memory and silent ruins. The citadel was called Zimbabwe or 'Great Place'. In 1980, the name was adopted by a modern country when its people won independence from the colonial British state of Rhodesia and became the republic of Zimbabwe. We have no records of the old kingdom and it collapsed before the arrival of the Europeans. What has survived are the granite stone walls of a silent city.

The Bantu people moving southwards from central Africa arrived in the area around the 1st century CE, bringing agriculture and also the knowledge of making iron. By the 13th century

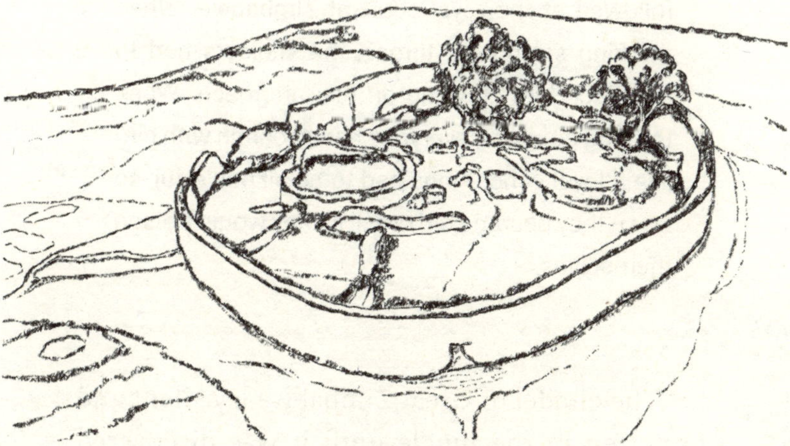

The ruins of the fortress at Great Zimbabwe

CE, the kingdom of Zimbabwe had been built by the Shona tribe. It covered modern Zimbabwe, Mozambique, Botswana and parts of modern South Africa and it seems to have prospered for two centuries until mysteriously vanishing. What remains are the ruins of a massive fortress called Great Zimbabwe built with thick stone walls on top of a hill with palaces, burial sites and temples that were built between the 11th and 16th centuries. It was the centre of a trading empire called Monomatapa.

Cough! Cough!

There are legends of the fascinating etiquette followed at the royal court at Zimbabwe. When the king sat on the throne, the subjects had to approach him crawling on their stomach. When the king coughed, everyone had to cough with him like a loyal echo. Kings had to be all powerful, so when they became old or fell ill they would poison themselves.

The citadel of Great Zimbabwe lay silent and forgotten in the jungle until it was discovered by Europeans who could not believe it had been built by Africans. They were convinced it had been built either by invading Arabs or even King Solomon of Israel because of the legend tied to the history of Ethiopia.

The city was built by stacking giant boulders and the fortress had stone towers and high walls. There must have been regular trade with the world as archaeologists have found Chinese pottery, Arabian glass and fragments of European textiles here. They calculate that at its peak it must have housed at least 20,000 people but no one knows why it was abandoned and never occupied again. The empty citadel was then taken over by the jungle and vanished from popular memory.

The Trade That Ruined Africa

Slavery has always existed in history but no continent has paid such a heavy price for it as the people of Africa. One of the reasons for Africa falling behind in many modern markers of development was this cruel and inhuman system where the youngest men and women of a society were made slaves and could not contribute to the progress of their own land. Historians calculate that over twelve million people were taken as slaves to the countries of North and South America between the 15th and 18th centuries, devastating a whole continent. How could Africa have progressed when millions of Africans were in chains?

Throughout history no one questioned the inhumanity of making human beings slaves. Slavery existed from the time of ancient China and Greece and most cities had markets where human beings were auctioned like goods. In Africa, the trade was first controlled by merchants from Arabia and the Ottoman Empire who took slaves to as far as India and China. Then in the 15th century the Portuguese arrived, followed by all other European countries and they kidnapped people in such large numbers that a whole continent was ruined for generations. Slave trading wars between

African kingdoms meant there was no peace in which a civilization could evolve. These were all military states and African soldiers and slave traders burned down villages, killed people and captured the young men and women leaving old people and children behind.

The earlier slave trade by Arabs was small in comparison to the European trade. Ships filled with people numbering in millions were taken across the Atlantic Ocean to work in the sugar and cotton plantations of the Unites States and South American countries like Brazil. Slaves in the east often worked in homes and were usually treated well. They had the right to gain freedom and in India we even had a dynasty of slave kings in Delhi. In Rome, many powerful bureaucrats were former slaves. The great Chinese explorer Zeng He was originally a slave.

However, it was a different picture in the United States and South America where they were treated as property with no rights and faced unimaginable cruelty. It took a civil war in the United States to free them. Also, we must not forget the role played by Africans in this as the slaves were supplied by African kings who grew rich from the trade.

AFRICA IS CALLING

- The capital of the kingdom of Kush was Meroe. The city stood on the east bank of the Nile, 200 kilometres from the modern city of Khartoum in Sudan. Around the site 200 pyramids have been excavated, much more than Egypt.
- One queen of Kush named Amanirenas defeated Roman forces in Egypt twice and came back with the head of a statue of Emperor Augustus. It was buried at the threshold of a temple so that people could walk over it.
- Around 700 CE a small civilization emerged in the Niger River Valley known as the Nok people. Very little is known about this rural community except for some eye-catching terracotta masks that we can now see in museums.
- No iron ploughs or wheels were used in ancient African kingdoms.
- The language spoken by the Bantu people is the root of many modern African languages. The tribe began a long trek from central Africa and took centuries to reach the south.
- In the middle ages, there was a popular legend in Europe of a mysterious Christian kingdom in

a remote part of Africa that was ruled by a king named Prester John and many explorers tried to find it. It was probably Ethiopia.

- Many travellers, including Ibn Batuta in 1353 and the Italian adventurer Leo Africanus, who mentions it in his book *Descrittione dell'Africa* (*Description of Africa*) published in 1550, visited the city of Timbuktu.
- Many Europeans explored Africa. The most famous was David Livingstone (1813–73) who made three journeys and crossed the continent following the Zambezi River seeking the source of the Nile. He discovered the Victoria Falls that he named after Queen Victoria of Britain.
- The kings of Ghana had an odd symbol of royalty: a golden stool that they said came down from heaven.
- The kingdom of Ghana included the region of Gambia, Guinea, Mali and Senegal but not the modern state of Ghana.
- The Ashanti were so rich they did not want any gold in exchange for slaves, so the Europeans sold them guns.
- The music created by African slaves is the origin of the musical styles of jazz and the blues of the United States.